ANSWERING THE WORLD

Core Jewish Values in the 21st Century

BY MOSHE PITCHON
21stCenturyJudaism.com

Answering the World: Core Jewish Values in the 21st Century
© 2026 Moshe Pitchon

Published in 2026
by 21stCenturyJudaism Publishing
United States of America
First edition

ISBN: 979-8-9948246-0-3 (print edition)

Scripture quotations are from standard Jewish and English translations unless otherwise noted.
Every effort has been made to identify and credit all sources. Any errors or omissions will be corrected in future editions.

This book is dedicated to my parents, Lina Covo and Rafael Pitchon—both war refugees who brought me into this world with a deep understanding of its complexities and challenges. From them I received not only life, but a quiet education in courage, responsibility, and hope. They did everything they could to give me the intellectual and human tools they believed I would need to help repair what is broken.

Their memory lives with me—not as something past, but as a continuing presence. I still feel their gaze upon me: a gaze shaped by love, understanding, and a gentle curiosity about who I was becoming in the world they had entrusted to me.

To you, my mother, and to you, my father, I offer only gratitude and admiration. May who I am stand as a reflection of who you were. I can imagine no greater tribute.

Contents

Foreword

I did not set out to write this book as an exercise in theology, nor as a defense of Jewish identity in the abstract. I wrote it because I have become increasingly aware of how unprepared many young Jews are to recognize false arguments, to answer growing antisemitism, or even to articulate what Judaism actually stands for.

Over the past years, I have written countless essays and blogs and published several books, all driven by the same concern: how Judaism speaks in a world shaped by accelerating technology, institutional fragmentation, and moral confusion. Again and again, I encountered the same pattern. Young people are intelligent, compassionate, and deeply concerned with justice—yet they are often disconnected from Judaism's own moral grammar. They are taught fragments of history, fragments of ritual, fragments of identity. What they rarely receive is Judaism as a coherent moral civilization: a tradition that trains human beings to remain answerable for their actions.

This gap has consequences. When Jewish values are reduced to cultural memory or political reflex, young Jews become vulnerable—not because they lack goodwill, but because they lack intellectual grounding. Without a living understanding of Judaism's core commitments—responsibility, dignity, justice, repair—they are left exposed to professionally packaged distortions that present hostility toward Jews or Israel as moral insight. What appears as ideological sophistication is often simply the absence of serious formation.

Judaism was never meant to be inherited passively. It is transmitted through study, argument, discipline, and lived responsibility. It assumes that human beings are moral agents whose choices matter, that freedom is inseparable from obligation, and that peace is not merely the absence of conflict but the restoration of human wholeness. These ideas do not survive by inertia. They must be taught, practiced, and renewed in every generation.

This book grows out of that conviction.

Its purpose is not nostalgia. It is not apologetics. It is an attempt to recover Judaism as a framework for moral agency in a world that increasingly diffuses responsibility across systems, technologies, and institutions. Drawing on biblical sources, rabbinic wisdom, and modern Jewish thought, I explore how Judaism holds together justice and compassion, truth and repair, individual conscience and communal obligation. I argue that Judaism offers something urgently needed today: a language for responsibility when accountability is being eroded, and a vision of human dignity when agency is being outsourced.

I have also come to believe that ideas alone are not enough. That is why this work is part of a broader effort to build intellectual infrastructure: publishing serious Jewish thought, creating spaces for learning and encounter, and developing educational programs aimed directly at young adults. The challenge before us is not merely cultural. It is formative. We must help the next generation acquire the moral clarity and inner strength required to meet the world as it is, not as we wish it to be.

Judaism teaches that we do not choose the conditions into which we are born—but we are responsible for how we answer them.

This book is my answer.

Rabbi Moshe Pitchon

Miami February 2026

Shevat 5786

Introduction

Are There Core Jewish Values?

Modern Jewish thought—religious and secular alike—has been marked by a persistent search for the essence of Judaism. Since the nineteenth century, philosophers and historians have repeatedly attempted to articulate an all-embracing formula capable of capturing what Judaism fundamentally is.

Despite early critiques—most notably by Franz Rosenzweig, who warned against the reductionism inherent in defining *Das Wesen des Judentums* ("the essence of Judaism"), and his criticism of Martin Buber for participating in this essentialist tendency—the impulse has endured. Secular scholars, liberal theologians, and Orthodox authorities alike have continued to seek Judaism's irreducible core.

Those who adopt this approach often speak of "normative Judaism," implying that beneath Judaism's historical diversity lies a hard, imperishable center, surrounded by peripheral ideas that may be modified or discarded. In this framework, Judaism is understood as possessing an objectively identifiable essence that must be preserved across time.

One influential version of this view appears in the work of Emil Fackenheim, who argued that Jewish philosophy combines a distinctive ethical message—rooted in the prophets of ancient Israel—with general philosophical method derived from Greek thought. Similar assumptions run through the scholarship of Julius Guttmann and Alexander Altmann, for whom Judaism's originality lay primarily in its ethical character.

This ethical emphasis finds early expression in rabbinic literature. Hillel the Elder, a first-century sage, famously summarized the Torah when asked by a would-be convert to explain it "while standing on one foot." His reply—often called the Golden Rule—was simple: *"What is hateful to you, do not do to your neighbor. That is the whole Torah; the rest is commentary."*

Two centuries later, Rabbi Akiva identified "You shall love your neighbor as yourself" as the Torah's central command. His contemporary Ben Azzai proposed instead a verse from *Bereshit* (the Book of Genesis-the first book of the Torah): *"This is the book of the generations of humanity... in the image of God He created them."* Ben Azzai thus grounded ethics not in emotion but in universal human dignity.

Rabbinic tradition continued this process of ethical condensation. The commandments given through Moses were symbolically reduced from 613 to eleven by King David, to six by the prophet Isaiah, to three by the prophet Micah, and finally to one by the prophet Habakkuk: *"The righteous live by faith."* These reductions were never intended to replace Torah observance, but to illuminate its moral center.

Christianity and Islam are creedal religions. Classical Judaism is not.

Ancient Judaism possessed shared theological convictions, but agreement about speculative theology was never imposed as a requirement of Jewish belonging. The Torah contains no verses beginning *"Thou shalt believe that...,"* and the Talmud formulates no formal articles of faith. In rabbinic usage, *emunah* -usually translated as "belief"- signifies trust and fidelity prior to doctrinal assent.

Although some modern thinkers claim that Judaism is simply a religion of law in which one may "believe whatever one wishes," this too oversimplifies. Judaism has always maintained foundational convictions. What it historically lacked was ecclesiastical machinery for enforcing creeds.

Lists of beliefs emerged only in the Middle Ages, largely under pressure from Christian and Islamic polemics. Saadia Gaon, Judah Halevi, and most famously Moses ben Maimon (Maimonides) attempted to articulate Judaism's foundations in systematic form. Maimonides' thirteen principles of faith, formulated in his commentary on the Mishnah, became the most influential of these efforts.

They were also sharply contested. Thinkers such as Joseph Albo, Crescas, and Isaac Abravanel rejected the idea that Judaism could be reduced to fixed dogmas. Abravanel argued explicitly that Judaism cannot be divided into essential and non-essential elements, since all commandments participate equally in covenantal life.

Later authorities narrowed Maimonides' thirteen principles to three; others expanded them; still others refused enumeration altogether. As Solomon Schechter observed, dogmas in Judaism function less as creeds than as indices—catalogues of ideas rather than boundaries of belonging.

Rabbi Leo Baeck later argued that Judaism lacks dogma in the strict sense because it never developed an authoritative institution empowered to impose doctrinal decrees. What Judaism enforces is practice, not belief.

In short: Judaism possesses foundational convictions, but the enforcement of dogma is alien to its core norms.

Modern historical scholarship further complicated the essentialist project. Some scholars sought Judaism's essence in original monotheism or language; others rejected any distinction between original and secondary elements. Still others located Judaism's essence in historical continuity itself. Figures such as Heinrich Graetz, Yitzhak Baer, and Gershom Scholem identified enduring patterns in Jewish consciousness—shared destiny, spiritual kinship, communal memory—recurring across historical peaks.

What emerges is not consensus but persistent disagreement.

Lowest common denominators may identify what all Judaisms share, but they cannot explain what makes any particular Judaism distinctive. They are necessary, but never sufficient.

This book therefore begins from a different premise.

Rather than asking whether Judaism can be reduced to an abstract essence, I ask whether Jewish civilization has sustained a continuous moral architecture—one that persists across textual, legal, historical, and cultural transformations.

These values emerge from *Bereshit* (the Book of Genesis), are dramatized in *Shemot* (the Book of Exodus), and are codified juridically in the *Talmud*—specifically in the tractate *Bava Kamma*, one of more than sixty tractates that form this vast rabbinic corpus.

Together they articulate a coherent anthropology: human beings possess intrinsic dignity (*b'tzelem Elohim*), are summoned into responsibility (*Hineni*), are shaped through liberation as moral formation, and remain accountable even under constraint (*adam mu'ad le-olam*).

My claim is not that Judaism can be distilled into a single doctrinal essence. It is that Judaism preserves a recognizable ethical trajectory. Forms of Judaism that deny human dignity, displace responsibility into systems, or sever freedom from obligation may retain Jewish symbols—but they rupture Judaism's moral continuity.

This book explores those core values not as dogma, but as the living conditions of Jewish moral life.

PART I:
FOUNDATIONS OF MORAL AGENCY

Chapter One

Hineni

What is Ethics, and Why Does Judaism Begin There?

Ethics is the disciplined question of how human beings ought to live—how we should act, what we may demand of one another, what we owe, what we must refuse, and what kind of person we are trying to become. It is not identical with law, custom, emotion, or social approval. A society can normalize cruelty; a community can bless injustice; an individual can feel righteous and still be wrong. Ethics begins precisely where we admit that we must answer not only to desire or power, but to a standard of right action that can judge us.

Judaism takes this question with unusual seriousness because it does not treat morality as an optional refinement added to religion. It treats ethical life as one of the ways human beings stand before reality itself: before God, before other persons, and before the consequences of what they do. Judaism is not "ethics alone," but it insists that without ethics—without restraint, obligation, truthfulness, and accountability—religion becomes spiritual theater.

Ritual may train the soul, law may structure a community, theology may give language to transcendence; but none of these can substitute for the moral demand that human beings be answerable for action.

This is why Jewish tradition repeatedly resists the notion that ethics is merely a private preference. The Torah does not ask only what a person believes, but what a person does. The prophets do not ask only whether a people worships, but whether it practices justice. Rabbinic literature does not treat virtue as sentiment, but as obligation expressed in concrete decisions. In Judaism, the moral life is not primarily a matter of self-expression; it is a matter of responsibility.

Responsibility is the central category because it connects ethics to human reality. It names the difference between a person and a force of nature. A storm causes harm; a person answers for harm. An animal acts; a person is accountable. To speak of responsibility is to claim that human beings are not merely moved by pressures, needs, or systems, but remain capable of judgment—and therefore obligated to exercise it.

This chapter begins with that claim and follows its consequences. It asks what Judaism means when it insists that responsibility precedes freedom, that dignity cannot be reduced to utility, and that accountability cannot be delegated to institutions, procedures, or technologies. In an age increasingly tempted to explain away agency—by psychology, by bureaucracy, by algorithm—Judaism's first ethical word remains uncompromising: you are answerable.

Collective Responsibility: From Covenant to Community

Responsibility in Judaism is never confined to the isolated self. The individual is accountable, but never alone. From its earliest formulations, Jewish ethics insists that persons exist within a web of mutual obligation.

The Mekhilta interprets the verse *"You shall be to Me a kingdom of priests and a holy nation"* as teaching that Israel is *one body and one soul*: when one part suffers, all are implicated. The Talmud codifies this intuition with stark clarity: all Israel are guarantors for one another. Responsibility is reciprocal, not optional.

This principle extends beyond legal culpability into moral solidarity. Judaism therefore cultivates not only individual conscience but social conscience. One is judged not merely by personal conduct but by willingness to intervene when others are harmed. Silence in the face of injustice is itself a form of participation.

At the same time, Judaism rejects both moral solipsism and tribal self-enclosure. Israel's covenantal identity was never conceived as an inward-looking privilege. From Sinai onward, Jewish peoplehood was bound to a universal horizon. The calling was to become a *kingdom of priests*—a community whose way of life would illuminate what human responsibility looks like in practice.

Rabbi Samson Raphael Hirsch expressed this mission succinctly: Israel was to become *a nation to which other nations have only to look in order to recognize their own task.*

This is why Jewish responsibility cannot terminate at communal boundaries. Rabbi Leo Baeck insisted that every human being bears an inviolable claim upon us simply by virtue of being human. Moral obligation precedes affiliation.

Judaism thus sustains a productive tension: loyalty to one's own people is inseparable from accountability to humanity.

Evading Responsibility

The tradition also understands how relentlessly human beings attempt to escape this burden.

Adam, the first human being, hides[1]; the prophet Jonah flees[2]. The modern world offers infinitely subtler hiding places: professional specialization, bureaucratic diffusion, technological mediation, distraction, exhaustion. We learn to confuse identity with identification—

---

1   Genesis 3:8–10 (especially v. 10: "I heard Your voice in the garden... and I hid.")

2   *Jonah* 1:3 ("But Jonah rose to flee to Tarshish from the presence of the Lord.")

mistaking credentials, accounts, and profiles for presence.

The Talmud warns that even one who does no direct harm fails morally if he refuses to serve others. To say *what is mine is mine and what is yours is yours*[3] is described as the character of Sodom. Justice requires engagement.

On the surface, *"what's mine is mine, what's yours is yours"* sounds fair—even civilized. But the rabbis label this stance *middat Sedom* ("the trait of Sodom") because of what it *refuses*.

In rabbinic thought, Sodom represents a society that:

- treats strict property rights as absolute,
- denies mutual obligation,
- withholds help even when helping costs nothing, and
- organizes itself so that no one is responsible for anyone else.

In other words, Sodom is the paradigm of moral isolationism.

The problem is not ownership; Judaism fully recognizes private property. The problem is the declaration: *I owe you nothing.* A community built on that principle collapses the idea of covenantal responsibility. It replaces solidarity with indifference.

That is why the sages associate this attitude with Sodom: not because it steals, but because it *refuses to care.*

Sodom symbolizes a world where people retreat behind boundaries—legal, economic, or institutional—and thereby escape answerability. It is an early model of systems that permit human beings to say, *"the system did it,"* or *"not my responsibility."*

"Sodom" signifies: a social order that preserves rights while extinguishing responsibility.

Responsibility, Judaism teaches, does not arise from voluntary generosity. It precedes choice. One is summoned before one consents.

As one rabbinic passage recounts, a dying sage weeps—not because of

---

3   Pirkei Avot 5:10

sins committed, but because he had the capacity to serve as a judge and declined. The fear is not transgression alone, but abdication.

The first divine question in Scripture—*Ayeka? Where are you?*[4]—continues to echo. It asks whether we are present to the demands placed upon us, or whether we have learned to disappear.

---

4   Genesis 3:9

Chapter Two

God

Judaism does not begin with proofs of God. It begins with a way of living.

The Hebrew Bible never commands belief in God. It commands action: justice, compassion, fidelity, responsibility. God enters Jewish life not as a speculative hypothesis but as the ultimate point of reference by which human life is measured and directed.

To speak of God in Judaism is therefore not to describe an object among other objects. God is not a thing in the world. God is that in relation to which the world itself becomes intelligible.

In Jewish experience, God names the reality that calls human beings beyond themselves — beyond instinct, beyond power, beyond convenience. God is not encountered as an abstract metaphysical entity but as a summons: a demand for accountability, a claim upon conscience, a horizon of meaning.

This is why idolatry is Judaism's central danger. Idolatry occurs whenever finite realities — nation, ideology, wealth, power, even religion itself — are mistaken for ultimate reality. To affirm God is to deny that any human institution or individual can be absolute.

God sets limits on human narcissism.

In the Bible, God is known through relationship, not definition.

God speaks. Humans answer. Humans argue. God responds. The Torah records a living dialogue: Abraham challenges divine justice, Moses negotiates on behalf of Israel, prophets protest God's silence. Jewish faith is forged not through submission alone but through engagement.

God, in this sense, is not primarily a cosmic explanation but a moral presence.

Judaism holds together two tensions without resolving them.

God is utterly beyond human comprehension — infinite, unnameable, mysterious. Yet God is also near — present in history, responsive to human action, addressed in prayer.

These are not contradictions to be solved. They are poles to be maintained.

If God becomes only transcendent, religion dissolves into abstraction.

If God becomes only immanent, God collapses into human projection.

Jewish thought insists on both: God is radically other and intimately involved.

This tension protects faith from fanaticism and from emptiness.

Biblical language speaks of God as personal: loving, judging, forgiving, commanding. These metaphors matter. They shaped Judaism's moral vision and helped generate ideas of human dignity, responsibility, and rights.

Yet Jewish philosophy insists that God is not literally a person. Personality is a metaphor drawn from human experience, used because no higher language is available.

To call God personal means: God is not an impersonal force. God addresses and is addressed. God enters relationship.

But God also exceeds every image.

Hence the tradition of negative theology: we say what God is not, knowing that every positive statement falls short.

Every statement about God is an understatement.

Across its many formulations, Judaism converges on one core function of God:

God is the ultimate point of reference.

God names that reality in light of which all values are judged, all power relativized, all claims held accountable.

To orient life toward God is to accept that no human perspective is final. It introduces humility into conviction. It opens space for repentance. It resists absolutism.

God functions as the critical center outside ourselves by which we may judge ourselves.

This is why Jewish faith is inherently self-critical.

The *brit* (the biblical covenant) is not a contract between ruler and subjects. It is a partnership. God commits to humanity. Humanity commits to God.

Remarkably, Jewish tradition teaches that God limits divine power in order to make room for human freedom. Responsibility is transferred to human hands. Law is interpreted by human courts. Moral decisions belong to people.

Judaism rejects religious passivity. God does not replace human agency; God summons it. A famous Talmudic story declares: "It is not in heaven,"[5] a striking episode *where* Rabbi Eliezer, defending his legal position, calls upon miracles to support his view. When these signs fail to persuade the other sages, a heavenly voice declares that Rabbi Eliezer is correct.

Then Rabbi Joshua rises and counter argues with a verse from the book of *Devarim* (*Deuteronomy*) *"It is not in heaven"*[6]. Since Torah was given at Sinai, he explains, its interpretation no longer belongs to Heaven but

---

5 This refers to one of the most famous passages in the Talmud (Babylonian Talmud, *Bava Metzia* 59b), known as *the Oven of Akhnai*.

6 *Deuteronomy* 30:12

to human beings, who are commanded to decide by majority judgment. The Talmud adds that God Himself responds with delight: *"My children have defeated Me."*

The meaning is unmistakable. Judaism refuses to outsource moral and legal responsibility—even to God. Revelation does not abolish human judgment; it inaugurates it.

This passage establishes a radical Jewish principle: Once Torah enters human history, *responsibility for interpretation belongs to human beings*. Not miracles; not heavenly voices; not charismatic authority. Judaism insists that moral and legal judgment must be exercised *here*, by accountable persons, through argument, community, and majority decision.

This is one of Judaism's clearest declarations that responsibility cannot be outsourced — not even to God. Creation itself becomes incomplete without human participation.

The Evolution of how God in seen in Jewish History

There is no single Jewish doctrine of God.

Biblical anthropomorphism gives way to philosophical abstraction. Medieval rationalism meets mystical pantheism. Covenant theology confronts catastrophe after the Holocaust. Feminist theology challenges patriarchal images. Contemporary thought struggles with divine silence.

Judaism survives because it allows reinterpretation. Every generation must rearticulate God in light of new knowledge, new suffering, new responsibility.

Jewish theology today must confront divine absence as seriously as divine presence. The Holocaust shattered naive providentialism. God did not intervene.

This forces a deeper truth: God does not act instead of humanity. God acts through humanity — or not at all. Responsibility cannot be deferred upward.

Judaism ultimately understands God not as a substitute for moral action but as its ground. God does not absolve responsibility; God creates it.

To believe in God is to accept that the world is entrusted to us. Creation becomes a task. Justice becomes an obligation. Compassion becomes command.

God is not the solution to human problems. God is the reason humans must solve them.

Chapter Three

In God's image

The biblical declaration that the human being is created *b'tzelem Elohim*—in the image of God[7]—is among the most consequential sentences in moral history. It introduces a claim Judaism treats as axiomatic: that every human life possesses intrinsic and equal worth, independent of status, power, intelligence, or usefulness.

Yet the Torah does not present the divine image as a metaphysical "thing" lodged in human substance. Genesis speaks less about what a human being *is* in isolation than about what occurs when God creates a being capable of address, response, and accountability. The image is therefore better understood as *a calling and a capacity*—a potentiality given with our very being—rather than a fixed endowment that can be measured, ranked, or lost by degree.

Jewish interpretation consistently resists reducing *tzelem Elohim* to a single faculty such as reason, consciousness, dominion, or creativity. Some thinkers emphasized intellect; others, freedom; others, relationality and communication; others, the power to rule or to generate life. But the tradition converges on a practical center of gravity: the image becomes visible primarily in conduct. Human beings do not become God. They cannot cross the boundary between creature and Creator. But their behavior can be Godlike—merciful, just, faithful, protective of life.

---

7   *Genesis* 1:27

This is why *tzelem Elohim* functions as a *"basic norm"*[8] in Jewish ethics and law: it does not need to be justified by something deeper.

Because each person bears God's image, human life becomes the supreme value, the pivot of civil and capital law, and the ground of obligations toward the vulnerable, the stranger, and even the enemy. The image is not theological ornament. It is the foundation of a moral and legal architecture of responsibility.

In an age tempted to redefine humanity in the image of its own machines, *b'tzelem Elohim* stands as a counter-anthropology. It insists that dignity precedes performance, and that persons are not data points, products, or systems to be optimized, but beings who can answer— who are summoned into moral life before they ever "choose" it.

Read this way, *tzelem Elohim* is not a compliment but a burden—an elevation that immediately becomes obligation. If the image is realized in action, then it is realized wherever a person can be held answerable: in speech, restraint, care, fidelity, judgment. That is why Genesis does not merely confer dignity; it establishes a framework of responsibility in which the human being is the one creature who must respond to more than appetite, impulse, or utility. To be created in God's image is to be placed under the demand to "answer" for what one does to life—one's own, and the life of the other. And this is precisely the point

---

8   Basic norm (*Grundnorm* in German) is a term from legal philosophy introduced by Hans Kelsen. It means the foundational, presupposed rule that gives validity to an entire legal system. In Kelsen's theory, no law stands on its own. Every rule gets its authority from a higher rule—until you reach a final, unprovable starting point. That ultimate starting point is the *Grundnorm*. It isn't written in any statute. It's the assumed principle that lets us treat a system of rules as binding at all (for example: *"the constitution ought to be obeyed"*).
Modern legal systems locate their *Grundnorm* in constitutions or sovereign authority. Judaism, by contrast, locates it in responsibility itself—in covenant, in *Hineni*, in *b'tzelem Elohim*. Authority does not terminate in power or procedure, but in the human obligation to answer. So where Kelsen's *Grundnorm* is a formal presupposition of legality, Judaism's "basic norm" is moral: *the human being is answerable*.

at which the modern crisis returns: when agency is dispersed and accountability is outsourced, the erosion is not only social or political; it is an erosion of the image itself, because it is an erosion of the human capacity—and duty—to say, in truth, *hineni*: here I am.

PART II:
FORMATION OF THE MORAL SELF

Chapter Four

Torah

Torah does not mean "law" in the narrow legal sense. That misunderstanding—cemented when the Greek translators rendered Torah as nomos—has distorted Judaism for over two millennia. Torah means instruction. It signifies teaching, guidance, formation.

In its earliest biblical usage, Torah referred to concrete acts of instruction: a parent teaching a child, a priest guiding a worshiper, a prophet addressing a community, a sage offering counsel. Only later did the term come to designate written collections of teachings. Originally, Torah was oral, relational, and practical. It belonged to the lived world of human formation.

Even within the Bible itself, Torah never names a single fixed book. It designates specific priestly procedures, prophetic instruction, parental guidance, and eventually broader bodies of teaching. Only gradually—through the books of *Devarim* (*Deuteronomy*), *Ezra*, and the post-exilic period—did Torah become associated with a comprehensive written corpus. And only much later did it expand further to include prophetic writings, wisdom literature, rabbinic interpretation, and ultimately the entire sacred tradition of Judaism, both written and oral.

By late antiquity, Torah had become the collective name for the whole of Jewish teaching: *TaNaKh* (Scripture), *Mishnah*, *Talmud*, and continuing interpretation. In this sense, *Torah is not a document. It is a formative way of life, organizing memory, obligation, learning, and com-*

munal responsibility across time.

To speak of Torah, therefore, is to speak not merely of text but of transmission—of a living process in which teaching passes from generation to generation through study, debate, ritual, and practice. Torah names a relationship between past and present, between revelation and responsibility.

This is why classical Judaism insists that Torah must be both studied and enacted. One does not merely possess Torah; one *does* Torah. Although the word never appears grammatically as a verb, its meaning is inseparable from action. Learning Torah obligates response. Knowledge without practice is incomplete.

This dynamic understanding also explains why Judaism preserved such a striking plurality of voices within its sacred literature. The Hebrew Bible (the *TaNaKh*) is not a harmonized system. It contains competing ideologies, conflicting historical interpretations, divergent theological emphases, and unresolved tensions. Priestly, prophetic, royal, wisdom, and popular traditions stand side by side. Editors did not erase contradictions; they curated them. *This was not a failure of coherence. It was a philosophical choice.*

The compilers recognized that truth cannot be reduced to a single perspective. God speaks in many voices, and human beings hear in many ways. Rather than imposing uniformity, the biblical editors assembled a pluralistic canon capable of sustaining continuous inquiry. Torah thus became not a closed doctrine but an open field of moral reasoning. *Judaism emerged not as a religion of settled answers but as a tradition of disciplined questioning.*

Equally important is the fact that Torah never exists apart from community. A book alone does not create a people. Judaism did not arise because individuals read Scripture and agreed with it. Judaism arose because Israel existed as a social entity, bound together by memory, ritual, law, and shared responsibility. The text both shaped that community and was shaped by it.

Synagogue and study house preserved Torah—but Torah also preserved synagogue and people. Across centuries of exile and dispersion, it provided continuity not merely through words, but through practices: prayer, law, ethical formation, and communal obligation.

This also explains why Torah cannot be reduced to literalism. Jewish tradition never treated Scripture as self-interpreting. Meaning emerges through generations of commentary, disagreement, and lived experience. Even divine authority does not abolish human judgment.

Torah therefore functions not as an infallible instruction manual but as a formative framework. It shapes conscience. It trains judgment. It cultivates responsibility.

Its authority does not rest primarily in claims about authorship or inerrancy. It rests in its capacity to generate moral persons and sustainable communities. Torah becomes authoritative when it forms human beings capable of answering for their actions. This is why Torah is inseparable from responsibility.

The sages expressed this insight with striking clarity: God created the world for the sake of Torah. This does not mean that reality exists to obey rules. It means that civilization itself depends on teaching, transmission, and moral formation. Torah represents ordered meaning against chaos. It offers a shared language through which individuals cross from private impulse into interhuman accountability.

In this sense, Torah stands not for legalism but for coherence. It provides the grammar of a moral world.

Yet Torah is also brutally honest. The Bible does not idealize its heroes. It exposes betrayal, rebellion, failure, and moral collapse. Israel's history is presented as a continuous struggle between divine demand and human resistance. No other ancient literature makes national apostasy its central theme. Torah does not flatter its people; it educates them.

This honesty is essential. Torah teaches that moral life is not inherited automatically. Each generation must relearn responsibility. Each community must re-enter the covenant consciously. Each individual must decide whether to answer.

Torah thus remains unfinished.

It is renewed every time it is studied seriously, argued passionately, and enacted faithfully. It survives not because it is ancient, but because it continues to form human beings who accept the burden of judgment.

And this is precisely why Torah matters now.

Torah, however, does not exist in abstraction.

Instruction requires a people. Teaching presupposes learners. Covenant demands a community capable of memory, continuity, and response. Torah becomes real only when embodied in a living society.

That society is Israel.

Israel is not merely a historical nation or a religious category. It is the social form Torah takes in the world. Without Israel, Torah would remain a collection of texts and ideals. Without Torah, Israel would be just another people among peoples. Together, they constitute a singular experiment in moral history: a community organized around responsibility rather than power, remembrance rather than conquest, obligation rather than entitlement.

Israel emerges in the Bible not as a finished identity but as a continual becoming. It is shaped through exile and return, failure and repair, argument and recommitment. Again, and again, the tradition insists that belonging is not automatic. One does not inherit covenant biologically. One enters it through choice, learning, and action.

This is why Israel is best understood not as ethnicity alone, nor as creed alone, but as a disciplined way of inhabiting history. It is a people formed by teaching, sustained by interpretation, and bound by mutual responsibility. Israel exists wherever Jews assume accountability for one another, transmit memory to their children, and translate inherited wisdom into present action.

Torah provides the grammar. Israel provides the voice. In every generation, that voice must decide whether it will speak.

The question is never whether Torah survives as text. The question is whether Israel survives as a moral community. That question leads us directly to the next chapter. For Israel is not defined by territory alone, or ancestry alone, or belief alone. Israel is defined by responsibility. And responsibility begins when a people accepts that its destiny is inseparable from its choices.

Chapter Five

Israel

Israel Before Territory

Israel does not originate as a state, nor even as a land. It begins as a summons.

Before borders, sovereignty, or geography, there is obligation. Abraham is called away from origin toward responsibility. Israel emerges not through conquest but through response. This ordering is decisive: Jewish identity is not inherited passively but entered through moral commitment. The covenant precedes territory.

Significantly, the Torah concludes with Moses outside the land. Revelation is completed before possession. Instruction comes before settlement. Israel first exists as a people bound by obligation. Only afterward does it become a people in a place.

The structure itself teaches that land without responsibility is empty, while responsibility without land remains incomplete.

Land as Trust, Not Property

Biblical tradition consistently resists describing the land as Israel's possession. *"The land is Mine,"*[9] declares God; Israel is depicted as resident alien rather than owner. The land is given in trust, not seized as entitlement.

This distinction shapes Jewish political consciousness.

Territory is not absolute. Presence is conditional. The land is sustained by justice and forfeited by corruption. Scripture repeatedly insists that displacement follows moral failure: the land itself "vomits out" those who violate its ethical order.

In Judaism, geography is inseparable from conduct. The soil responds to behavior.

No idea recurs more persistently than conditionality.

The fifth book of the Torah- Devarim (*Deuteronomy*)- makes explicit that prosperity depends on obedience, security on justice, and continuity on restraint. Sovereignty carries no inherent sanctity. Military success bears no theological guarantee. Kings who expand borders without righteousness leave little imprint on Jewish memory, while prophets who defend the vulnerable shape its conscience.

Holiness emerges from action, not acquisition. The land becomes sacred only through the way a people inhabits it.

Israel's distinctiveness lies not only in return but in survival without sovereignty.

For nearly two millennia, Jews maintained a civilization without territory, anchored instead in law, ritual, memory, and study. Exile did not dissolve Jewish identity; it refined it. Political power vanished, yet communal responsibility endured.

At the same time, Jewish tradition never normalized homelessness. Return remained embedded in prayer, liturgy, and historical imagination. Israel learned to live everywhere while belonging somewhere.

This tension—between dispersion and destination—formed Judaism's

---

9   Leviticus 25:23

enduring consciousness.

The Modern State: Responsibility Reintroduced

The establishment of the State of Israel in 1948 marked a civilizational turning point. For the first time in modern history, Jews assumed comprehensive responsibility for public life: governance, security, economy, and social order. Judaism moved from minority ethics to majority ethics, from endurance to accountability. This transition is unprecedented.

Israel is not merely refuge or homeland. It is a moral experiment: can Jewish values shape political power? Can covenantal responsibility survive sovereignty? Can compassion persist under conditions of force?

The state does not consummate redemption. It inaugurates responsibility.

Israel is best understood not as theological fulfillment but as historical trial.

When land replaces covenant, Judaism is distorted.

Territorial absolutism transforms geography into idol. Mystical nationalism confuses possession with holiness. Political success is misread as divine sanction. This represents not continuity but regression.

Jewish tradition insists otherwise: land is instrumental, not ultimate. Its sanctity derives from justice, restraint, and care for the vulnerable. Detached from these, territory becomes indistinguishable from any other.

The prophets warned repeatedly against this confusion. Their warning remains current.

Israel today embodies both promise and fragility: technological achievement alongside social division; military strength alongside moral vulnerability; cultural creativity alongside ideological polarization.

This is not accidental. Judaism never imagined redemption without risk.

Israel exists to demonstrate whether a society can be organized around responsibility rather than domination—toward minorities, strangers, neighbors, and future generations.

That is Israel's enduring meaning. Not perfection. Responsibility.

Chapter Six

Moral grammar

The land gathers bodies; language gathers consciousness. Israel is not sustained by territory alone. A people does not endure through borders, armies, or institutions. It endures through memory—and memory requires language.

If Israel is the ethical experiment of Jewish history, Hebrew is its operating system.

The covenant entered history through words. Creation itself unfolds through speech. Law is transmitted as teaching. Prophecy speaks before it commands. Even exile was survived linguistically: through prayer, study, and recitation. Long before modern sovereignty was restored, Hebrew preserved continuity across dispersion.

Hebrew does more than communicate. It shapes perception. Its verbs carry moral direction. Its nouns encode relationship. Its grammar reflects responsibility. In Hebrew, to know is to be bound; to hear is to obey; to remember is to act. This is why Jewish civilization could survive without territory but not without text.

The return to Israel in the twentieth century therefore required more than political reconstruction. It demanded linguistic resurrection. Hebrew had to be brought back from liturgy into life, from prayer into policy, from scripture into streets.

Hebrew is not merely the language Jews speak. It is the language Jews think in.

Every civilization carries its moral assumptions inside its grammar. Words do not simply describe reality; they shape it. They carry histories, values, and hidden metaphysics. For Judaism, Hebrew is not a neutral vehicle of communication. It is the medium through which Jewish consciousness itself was formed.

Any language other than Hebrew comes already burdened with the cultural and religious residues of the civilization that produced it. Translation is always an approximation. Something essential is lost, and something foreign is inevitably added. Hebrew concepts do not migrate cleanly into Greek, Latin, German, English, French or Spanish. Each substitution subtly alters meaning.

This is why Jewish ideas so often appear distorted when filtered through external philosophical systems. In Hebrew, to *know* is not merely to possess information; it implies intimacy and responsibility. To *hear* means to respond. To *remember* is to act. Language encodes obligation.

Hebrew is therefore not only descriptive. It is directive.

Judaism enters history through speech. Creation unfolds through divine utterance. Covenant is sealed through words. Law is transmitted as teaching. Prophecy speaks before it commands. Even exile was survived linguistically: through prayer, study, recitation, and argument. Long before political sovereignty was restored, Hebrew sustained continuity across dispersion. The land gathers bodies. Language gathers consciousness. This is why Jewish civilization could endure without territory but not without text.

The modern revival of Hebrew was therefore not merely a cultural achievement. It was a civilizational event.

For nearly two millennia, Hebrew lived primarily in liturgy and learning. It was the language of prayer, of study, of commentary and argument. It was not spoken casually in marketplaces or playgrounds.

Then, in the twentieth century, Hebrew was brought back into daily life. It moved from synagogue to street, from scripture to policy, from sacred page to public square. This transformation carried enormous power—and enormous risk.

Already in 1926, Gershom Scholem warned of what this linguistic resurrection entailed. He observed that Hebrew could not be safely secularized. Its words, he wrote, were "laden with explosives." Every expression drawn from its ancient treasury carried accumulated layers of sacred invocation. Hebrew had been used for centuries to address God, to plead for redemption, to articulate messianic hope. To assume that such a language could be emptied of its theological charge was an illusion.

Scholem feared that Zionism believed it had neutralized Hebrew's spiritual potency by repurposing it for modern political life. He argued the opposite: that by returning Hebrew to everyday use, Jews were re-activating dormant forces whose consequences could not be predicted or controlled. God, he warned, would not remain silent in a language that had so long been used to summon divine presence. His concern was not mystical alarmism. It was moral realism.

Hebrew does not forget its past. Its vocabulary carries covenantal memory. Its syntax reflects responsibility. Its letters themselves have been treated as vessels of meaning. To revive Hebrew is to reintroduce an entire moral universe into public life.

This is why attempts to replace religious meaning with purely political meaning are ultimately unstable. The language resists confinement. It reasserts depth where superficiality is imposed. It carries expectations that exceed ideology.

Hebrew remembers what its speakers try to forget.

Modern Israel did not merely rebuild cities and institutions. It reconstructed a linguistic civilization. This act restored Jewish agency—but it also reopened unresolved theological questions. What happens when a language shaped by prophecy and covenant becomes the language of bureaucracy, military command, and parliamentary debate? What does responsibility mean when sacred words govern secular power? These questions cannot be avoided. They are embedded in every sentence spoken in Hebrew today.

Unlike Western political languages, Hebrew does not arise from Enlightenment social contract theory or Roman legalism. It arises from covenant. Its basic grammar presupposes relationship rather than autonomy. It does not begin with individual rights but with mutual obligation. It does not imagine humans as isolated agents but as participants in inherited responsibility.

This is why Hebrew resists purely instrumental use.

To speak Hebrew is to inhabit a moral structure whether one intends to or not.

The revival of Hebrew thus represents something unprecedented: an ancient ethical language reentering modern statehood. No other civilization has attempted such a fusion. Greek did not return with Athens. Latin did not govern Rome again. Hebrew alone made this journey—from revelation to exile to resurrection.

And with that return comes accountability. Language shapes judgment. Judgment shapes action. Action shapes history. Together they determine whether responsibility becomes justice—or merely authority.

Chapter Seven

Family

Judaism does not begin in the synagogue. It begins in the home.

Long before Jews possessed political sovereignty, institutional power, or even a common spoken language, they possessed families. In exile, dispersion, and persecution, it was the household—not the state, not the clergy, and not even formal worship—that carried Jewish continuity forward.

Judaism taught Jews how to conduct family life. And family life, in turn, taught Jews how to live Judaism.

This reciprocal relationship is foundational. In the Jewish worldview, the family is not merely a private arrangement for companionship or reproduction. It is a moral institution: a network of reciprocal duties and obligations linking generations together. Parents are responsible for children; children are responsible for parents; spouses are bound to one another not only emotionally but covenantally.

The image of Judaism as a family-centered civilization took definitive shape during the exile. Deprived of land, sovereignty, and temple, Jews reorganized religious life around the household. What had once been reinforced by national institutions now depended on domestic transmission. The family became the primary vessel of identity.

In their extraordinary life without state or country, without army or government, dispersed among the nations and subject to repeated oppression, Jews made desperate efforts to preserve their uniqueness and the cultural and spiritual treasure they had inherited. In those efforts, the family served as a mighty fortress.

Despite common assumptions, the synagogue has never been the true center of Jewish life. The home has always held that role. Ritual, memory, education, and moral formation all begin at the kitchen table. Holidays are rehearsed through meals. Identity is transmitted through stories. Values are embodied in daily habits.

Judaism does not outsource formation.

This emphasis reflects something deeper. In biblical thought, the family—not the isolated individual—constitutes the basic building block of society. Ancient Israel organized itself through households, clans, and lineages. The vocabulary of relationship in the Hebrew Bible—father, mother, son, daughter, brother—also becomes the primary language for describing God's bond with Israel. Divine covenant is expressed through familial metaphors. Theology itself is shaped by domestic experience.

Many of Judaism's central moral intuitions emerge from this structure. Love is first learned in the family. Responsibility is practiced there before it is legislated. Authority is encountered not abstractly but personally. Even justice is experienced initially through parental fairness and sibling rivalry.

Saadia Gaon already argued that much of biblical moral legislation rests on preserving family structure. The continuity of covenant depends on generational transmission. Procreation and nurture are therefore not merely biological acts but sacred responsibilities. To raise children is to safeguard the future of a people.

Yet Judaism never romanticizes the family. It recognizes both its necessity and its limits.

Historical and contemporary evidence alike show that families cannot always meet the emotional, physical, or economic needs of their members. Jewish communities therefore developed extensive networks of mutual aid: burial societies, bridal funds, care for widows and orphans, communal charity. These institutions testify to a profound insight: family responsibility extends outward into communal responsibility.

Judaism refuses to isolate the household. The family is foundational, but it is not sufficient.

This balance—between intimate obligation and collective care—has been essential to Jewish survival. It explains why Judaism places such emphasis on hospitality, charity, and mutual support. No household stands alone.

The tradition also affirms marriage as normative, not out of sentimentality, but because partnership stabilizes responsibility. The rabbis speak bluntly: without family, joy, blessing, and peace are diminished. Singleness is not condemned, but covenantal companionship is preferred. Judaism resists spiritualizing solitude.

Even so, family authority is never absolute. Parents possess great responsibility, but their power is constrained by Torah. Abuse, favoritism, and cruelty are prohibited. The Bible itself exposes family conflict with startling honesty: sibling rivalry, betrayal, parental blindness, generational fracture. Joseph is sold by his brothers[10]. Moses is rejected by his people[11]. No lineage is idealized. Scripture refuses to sanitize domestic life.

This honesty is itself instructive. The family is not presented as a haven of perfection but as the primary arena of moral struggle. It is where love is tested, forgiveness practiced, patience learned, and responsibility enforced. The family teaches realism.

After the destruction of the Second Temple in 70 CE, the family again absorbed functions once carried by national institutions. With sacrifice gone and priesthood displaced, Judaism retreated into homes and

10   *Genesis* 37:26–28

11   *Exodus* 2:13–14

study halls. Identity survived because it had already been decentralized. Text and table replaced altar and throne. Family became portable civilization.

Today, in an age of accelerating individualism and technological mediation, this legacy faces unprecedented pressure. Digital culture weakens intergenerational bonds. Economic mobility scatters households. Artificial intelligence threatens to replace care with automation and presence with efficiency.

Yet Judaism insists: responsibility cannot be outsourced to systems. Children require presence, not algorithms. Elders require dignity, not optimization. Love requires time. Memory requires transmission. No technology can substitute for covenant. Family remains Judaism's first school of responsibility.

And this is why the family stands at the center of Jewish moral architecture. It is where values are embodied before they are articulated. It is where freedom first encounters obligation. It is where the abstract ideals of Torah become lived reality.

Chapter Eight

Jewish Learning

Chapter 7 showed why Judaism could survive without territory or power: the home became a fortress of identity, a small jurisdiction of duty, intimacy, and transmission. But a fortress can still become a museum. A home can preserve warmth and memory while losing clarity, vocabulary, and rigor. The Jewish home survives only when it is paired with a second institution—one that trains not only attachment, but understanding: education.

Judaism did not treat education as a luxury for the gifted or the wealthy. It treated learning as a covenantal obligation—an act that binds generations, equalizes social standing, and disciplines conscience. A people can survive poverty, migration, even political collapse. But it cannot survive the loss of teaching.

The classic biblical command is not only to believe, but to teach—"*when you sit at home and when you walk on the road, when you lie down and when you rise up*[12]." The instruction is continuous, woven into ordinary time. Judaism does not imagine education as a phase one outgrows. It is not something you "complete." Graduation, in this sense, is an oxymoron. One becomes a person by becoming a learner, and remains a person by remaining teachable.

Universal literacy is a modern Western ideal, but Jewish society treat-

---

12   Deuteronomy 6:7; Deuteronomy: 11:19

ed basic education as a communal duty long before modern states did. This is not a romantic claim; it is a structural one. Judaism is a religion of texts and a civilization of interpretation. Once a tradition locates holiness in words—law, narrative, instruction, blessing—education becomes the very mechanism of continuity.

That is why rabbinic Judaism could rule, already in late antiquity, that a community that fails to establish schooling places itself outside the moral boundaries of the collective[13]. It is also why, in moments of terror, Jews repeatedly protected schooling as a priority, even when everything else was collapsing. When Spanish Jewry faced persecution, expulsions, and ruin, it levied communal funds—taxes on food and life-cycle events—to ensure children would not be denied instruction. That is not sentimental piety. It is civilizational realism: if children lose literacy, a people lose the future.

Judaism makes education "democratic" in a deeper sense: it refuses the idea that moral knowledge can be monopolized by a priestly caste. The obligation placed upon everyone to study becomes a check against the corruption of the "anointed," the self-appointed owners of God's will. Where religion creates elites without accountability, it rots. Judaism's answer is astonishingly simple: distribute the sources, teach the people, and require the powerful to safeguard the learning of those who depend on them.

A famous rabbinic debate asks: which is greater, study or practice? The consensus is subtle: *study is greater because it leads to practice*[14]. The point is not that learning replaces action. It is that action without understanding becomes either habit or fanaticism—behavior that cannot explain itself, correct itself, or answer for itself.

In Judaism, study is not only preparation for ethics. It is part of ethics. It trains attention, patience, precision, and humility. It teaches the difference between impulse and judgment. It also protects a tradition

---

13 Talmud, Bava Batra 21a

14 Talmud, *Kiddushin* 40b.

from becoming a fossil: without continuous learning, Judaism becomes a relic—an object of nostalgia rather than a lived discipline.

A responsible person is not merely sincere. He is answerable. And answerability requires language, concepts, sources, and memory. Education is the infrastructure of moral agency.

Jewish learning, even when anchored in writing, is deeply oral. The verbs for "reading" in biblical cultures often carry the sense of calling out, speaking, proclaiming. Texts were "for the ears rather than the eyes." Torah is not simply absorbed privately; it is recited, repeated, argued, answered. That is why Judaism developed pedagogies of question and response, including what some scholars call "school questions" scattered through biblical wisdom literature and prophetic rhetoric.

This matters because it protects Judaism from a common modern distortion: treating education as the accumulation of information. Jewish learning is not merely cognitive. It is formative. It shapes character, habits of speech, patterns of self-restraint, capacities for empathy and gratitude. It is meant to form a human being who can live in covenant with others.

Jewish education begins in the home and never fully leaves it. Before schools, children learn core verses, blessings, and daily obligations aurally, through repetition and imitation. Even the child's earliest experiences—sweetness on the letters, honey on the words[15]—symbolize

---

15 The image of *"sweetness on the letters, honey on the words"* refers to an old Jewish educational custom practiced in parts of medieval Europe, Yemen, Kurdistan, and North Africa.

When a child began formal Torah study, the teacher would write Hebrew letters or short verses on a slate or parchment and smear them with honey. The child was invited to lick the letters while reciting them aloud. The custom consciously echoes the biblical image in Book of the prophet *Ezekiel* 3:1–3, where the prophet is commanded to *eat* a scroll containing God's words and finds it "sweet as honey." In later rabbinic imagination, this becomes a pedagogical principle: the child's first encounter with Torah should be physically pleasurable, establishing an association between learning and delight that precedes abstract understanding.

a central Jewish conviction: Torah is not external information; it is nourishment. One does not merely "know" it. One ingests it. It becomes part of the self.

Ritual itself is designed as pedagogy: the holidays teach time, memory, and meaning; life-cycle practices teach gratitude, fragility, and responsibility.

But Judaism is too honest to pretend the nuclear family can bear everything. Jewish communities historically created institutions—burial societies, mutual aid networks, charitable groups—that testify to a communal assumption: when families cannot support their members, the community must. Education follows the same logic. Parents are responsible, but communities are guarantors. A Jewish society that abandons schooling abandons its duty to the next generation.

When education becomes fear

In parts of pre-modern Europe, Jewish communities fell into contempt for "all learning," forbidding languages, mathematics, science, geography, and even much of Jewish philosophy and poetry. Whether one judges that account harshly or sympathetically, the underlying pattern is intelligible: under threat, communities sometimes protect identity by shrinking the world.

That strategy can preserve boundaries, but it also produces fragility. It yields a Judaism that survives by denial—a Judaism that fears knowledge as contamination. The result is not strength but brittleness: a tradition unable to speak credibly to reality, unable to equip its children for the world they must inhabit.

This is why modern Jewish education cannot be founded on a negation of modernity or a nostalgic return to the past. Jewish learning must be faithful to tradition while open to general culture. Catastrophic and redemptive events have always forced Jewish rebuilding. Education must be the place where Judaism remains intellectually alive—where it can render the world intelligible to mind and spirit without surrendering its moral core.

Modern Jewish institutions often treat education as a device to guarantee identity and continuity. The anxiety is understandable. The causal claim is not. Education can do many wonderful things, but it cannot manufacture souls. It cannot guarantee Jewish survival. It cannot "produce Jews" as if identity were an output of programming.

So what *can* Jewish education do?

It can provide the resources for the work each Jew must undertake to become—and keep becoming—Jewish. It can deepen literacy so Judaism is not left as a child's mythology. It can create serious encounter with texts, history, philosophy, prayer, ethics, and peoplehood. It can offer a peer community and a language of meaning. It can help a person live with dignity, responsibility, and belonging.

This is not a retreat from ambition. It is a rescue of education from propaganda. Education is not for social engineering. It is for human formation.

A tradition built on the sanctity of learning must confront the moral scandal of denying learning. The sacred image of the human being cannot be guarded by ignorance. Religious education, at its best, is precisely the practice of becoming aware of that sacred image.

A medieval proverb says: in prayer we speak to God; in study, God speaks to us [16]. This is not mystical poetry alone. It is a claim about the structure of Jewish religious life. Study is a mode of worship because it is an act of attention, submission to meaning, and willingness to be corrected. One can pray and still remain unchanged; one can study and be forced into argument with oneself.

That is why Judaism became, in a certain sense, a "religion of the intellect"—not because it worships intelligence, but because it treats under-

---

16 Hasidic saying, commonly attributed to R. Menachem Mendel of Kotzk (1787–1859).

standing as a moral duty. If human beings are co-workers with God, they must equip themselves for the task. They must learn the world and learn themselves.

Jewish education exists to form human beings capable of responsibility— toward God, toward others, toward truth, and toward the future.

It transmits texts and practices, yes. But it also transmits an attitude: a long tradition of truthful search, an abiding faith that human character is improvable, and a disciplined refusal to let moral life collapse into appetite, tribalism, or power.

It is not only education for survival. It is education for decency. And decency, in Judaism, is not softness. It is covenantal seriousness—the insistence that life is answerable.

PART III:
INNER VIRTUES AND
RELATIONAL ETHICS

Chapter Nine

Care Beyond Duty

Ḥesed (חֶסֶד) is one of the most untranslatable words in Jewish moral language. It is often rendered "lovingkindness" or "steadfast love," but the term carries more than warmth or generosity. At its core, Ḥesed names *love expressed as loyalty*—a beneficent response that arises from a binding relationship: family, friendship, covenant, host and guest, ruler and subject, the strong and the dependent. It is not mere sentiment. In Hebrew, Ḥesed includes both attitude and deed: the inner disposition and the concrete act that proves it.

That is why "kindness" can be too thin, and "mercy" too condescending. Ḥesed is not charity from above. It is readiness to come to another's aid, the moral reflex of a community held together by mutual obligation. It is "debt to be paid," not in the narrow sense of repayment, but in the deeper sense that a shared life creates responsibilities that cannot be shrugged off. Ḥesed is what keeps a bond from becoming a contract, and a covenant from becoming a legal fiction.

Biblical Hebrew often places Ḥesed as the object of the verb "to do"— to *do* Ḥesed. The concept is therefore inseparable from action.

English "loyalty" comes closer than "kindness," because it retains the element of commitment. Yet even "loyalty" falls short, because in modern usage it can imply blind obedience, or it can flow only upward (subordinate to superior). Biblical Ḥesed frequently moves in the opposite direction: *the powerful is loyal to the weak*, the secure to the vulnerable, the established to the stranger.

Ḥesed is love with backbone: steadfastness, persistence, and the willingness to stay bound when it would be easier to withdraw.

In the *TaNaKh* (Bible), Ḥesed is often associated with covenant (*berit*). This is not a technical detail; it is a moral idea. Covenant can degenerate into a mere agreement, each party reading the terms narrowly for self-protection. Ḥesed prevents that. It demands a surplus of faithfulness—behavior "beyond the letter"—so that covenant becomes a relationship capable of surviving strain, disappointment, and failure.

This is why the prophets can make Ḥesed the test of authentic religion. Hosea's famous claim—God desires Ḥesed more than sacrifice[17]—does not dismiss ritual; it insists that the point of worship is to produce a human being who can be relied upon. Ḥesed is the proof that covenant is not performance, but moral reality.

Jewish tradition distinguishes between *tzedakah* and *gemilut Ḥasadim* (deeds of Ḥesed). *Tzedakah* can be fulfilled by money. Ḥesed cannot. It asks not only for resources, but for presence: visiting the sick, comforting mourners, accompanying the dead to burial, welcoming guests, escorting them, rejoicing with bride and groom, noticing need before it becomes humiliation.

Tzedakah opens the hand. Ḥesed opens the person.

Jewish life is framed by the insistence that goodness is not an abstraction: it is embodied assistance at the vulnerable edge of existence.

Ḥesed is sometimes described as the virtue of excess—not excess as indulgence, but excess as *refusal to do only what is minimally required*. It is the capacity to act generously without turning the other into a project, a moral display, or a recipient of condescension. And it contains a further discipline: the ability to receive as well as give, so that giving does not become domination disguised as virtue.

---

17   *Hosea* 6:6 "For I desire Ḥesed and not sacrifice, knowledge of God rather than burnt offerings."

In this sense Ḥesed is not merely help; it is a moral style: a way of seeing people that searches for dignity rather than for grounds to dismiss them.

Jewish tradition frequently binds Ḥesed to *emet*—love to truth, compassion to integrity. This pairing prevents Ḥesed from becoming permissiveness, and prevents truth from becoming cruelty. Ḥesed without truth can become enabling; truth without Ḥesed can become violence. Together they form a mature moral posture: firmness that does not dehumanize, and care that does not lie.

A technological society can distribute aid efficiently and still fail at Ḥesed. Systems can process needs without ever *seeing* a person. But Ḥesed is precisely the act of turning toward the concrete human being in front of you—without asking first whether the person deserves it, whether it is optimal, or whether it can be automated.

This is why Ḥesed remains central to Jewish ethics. It is not a "soft" virtue. It is a covenantal discipline that binds a community together and trains the human being to place the focus of action outside the self. In a world increasingly mediated by institutions and machines, Ḥesed safeguards a basic truth: *human beings do not live by rights alone. They live by faithful care enacted in time.*

Chapter Ten

The Most Demanding Commandment

The Jews did not "discover" love in the ordinary sense. Every people has loved children, spouses, friends, and clan. What Judaism did—quietly, stubbornly, and with revolutionary consequences—was to *turn love into a moral and legal demand*, and to expand its horizon beyond instinct and tribe. Love becomes not only a feeling one happens to have, but a discipline one is commanded to practice: a way of seeing, judging, restraining oneself, and acting.

In the Torah, love is not a private emotion sealed inside the heart. It is a covenantal force meant to shape the social world.

In biblical Hebrew, *ahavah* (love) belongs to a whole constellation of terms that touch affection, loyalty, desire, attachment, and mercy. But *ahavah* has a distinctive moral weight. It can describe a father's love for a child, a person's love for another, and—most decisively—God's love for Israel. That last usage matters because it establishes the pattern: biblical love is not merely attraction. It is commitment expressed through responsibility.

Love in the Torah is never only a mood. It is a posture of fidelity.

One of the most important Hebraic intuitions is that love is bound to knowing. To "know" in Hebrew is not merely to register facts; it can mean intimacy, recognition, encounter, even union. This is why love cannot be reduced to sentimentality. One can only love what one is willing to truly see—to know in the sense of taking the other seriously, as a person and not a projection.

Love begins where fantasy ends: when the other is allowed to be real.

The commandment appears in its famous form: "*You shall love your neighbor as yourself—I am the Lord.*[18]" That final clause is not decorative. It is the axis. In Judaism, love of the other is not grounded in vague humanism alone. It is grounded in a claim about reality: the other stands before God, and therefore has a non-negotiable dignity.

And the Torah anticipates the human temptation: to make "neighbor" mean "my kind." So it immediately breaks the fence:

> *When a stranger lives with you in your land, do not mistreat him...*
> *Love him as yourself.*[19]

This is one of the Torah's most radical moral moves: it extends the grammar of love beyond kinship and nationality. The circle does not end at "us."

Many civilizations have praised love as an ideal. Judaism does something different: it legislates love—not because the Torah is naïve about feelings, but because it understands human beings. If love remains only an aspiration, it will be practiced when convenient and forgotten when costly. The Torah places love inside a dense world of concrete mitzvot—property law, wages, honesty, restraints on power, treatment of the vulnerable—so that love ceases to be poetry and becomes public responsibility.

This is why Rabbi Akiva can call love of neighbor "a great principle of the Torah"[20] And why Hillel can translate it into moral clarity: *do not do to another what you would not want done to you*[21]. Judaism turns

---

18 Leviticus 19:18

19 Leviticus 19:33–34

20 The classic source is *Sifra, Kedoshim* 4:12, where Rabbi Akiva comments on Leviticus 19:18 ("You shall love your neighbor as yourself"): A parallel version also appears in the Jerusalem Talmud (*Nedarim* 9:4), reinforcing the same teaching.

21 Babylonian Talmud, *Shabbat* 31a

love into a practical ethic of restraint, fairness, and attention to the needs of others.

In this tradition, love is not primarily what you feel. It is what you are willing to do. The phrase "as yourself" is not an invitation to sentimental equality. It is a demand to treat the other's good as real—urgent—binding. Love is tested precisely when it costs: when one must give time, status, comfort, ego, convenience. If love never interrupts your schedule, it is not yet a covenantal virtue; it is only preference.

Judaism's message is not that love replaces obligation. It is that obligation is one of love's most mature forms.

Chapter Eleven

Compassion without Sentimentality

If *hesed* is the love that keeps faith with a bond, *rahamim* is the love that responds to vulnerability. It is the Jewish refusal to treat suffering as background noise.

Judaism does not reduce compassion to a soft mood, nor does it romanticize it as weakness. *Rahamim* is a form of moral perception: the ability to see pain, to be moved by it, and to act in ways that preserve dignity.

And it is not optional. Jewish sources repeatedly insist that mercy is not an ornament of piety; it is one of the defining signs of a human being worthy of covenantal life.

Hebrew is unusually rich in the vocabulary of compassion: *rahamim*, *rahamanut*, *hemlah*, and related roots, along with verbs that mean to rescue, redeem, remember, help, and save. This is already a clue: Judaism thinks of compassion not as a single emotion, but as a whole moral field—a grammar of response.

Mercy is "absolute," a virtue in itself—not merely a reaction to what the recipient "deserves." In Jewish terms, that is exactly the point. Compassion is not a prize awarded to the worthy. It is a posture one takes before the exposed human condition.

Rehem (womb) and *rahamim* (compassion) share a root. The Torah and the rabbis know what modern moral psychology keeps rediscovering: compassion is the response we associate with the helpless—especially the child. It is *care directed toward dependency*, toward someone who cannot "pay back."

That womb-meaning is not merely poetic. It frames compassion as a kind of moral homecoming: *rahamim* is the impulse to draw the vulnerable back into protection—back toward life, shelter, recognition. That is why Jewish tradition can speak of remembering as mercy: to remember someone is to refuse their abandonment.

Judaism makes a daring claim: compassion is not only human; it is divine. God is called *HaRahaman*—"the Merciful"—and the human task is to imitate that divine quality in the social world. The moral logic is simple and severe:

- Compassion is how God relates to creation.
- Therefore compassion must become how Israel relates to human beings—and even to living creatures.

Jewish compassion is not restricted to the in-group. Sabbath rest for animals, the prohibition against muzzling an ox, the obligation to relieve an animal's burden—these laws train the heart by disciplining the hand. Compassion is not a theory. It is practice.

One of your strongest blocks is the Talmudic claim that mercy, modesty, and deeds of kindness are the three סימנים (signs) of the Jewish people—and of those fit to join them. That is not ethnic pride; it is moral diagnosis. It means:

A people cannot survive covenantal life if it becomes incapable of mercy.

And here Judaism adds an unsettling principle: compassion does not only respond to goodness; it responds to need. The widow, orphan, stranger, poor—these are not "causes." They are categories meant to expose the places where power preys on weakness. Compassion is the brake placed on human cruelty.

The fact that compassion is commanded does not make it mechanical;

it makes it dependable. The Torah does not command emotions in the modern romantic sense. It commands *forms of conduct* that reshape perception over time. You are not asked to "feel" mercy on cue. You are asked to act mercifully until mercy becomes part of your character.

This is why rabbinic sources can say: *"Man's compassion derives from God's compassion, but a man must first show compassion in order that the Lord should compassionate him."*[22] Mercy is contagious: it expands in a world that practices it, and it contracts in a world that mocks it.

The question is: How can justice be demanded and mercy be required without collapsing one into the other?

Judaism's answer is not a formula; it is a balance of imperatives:

- Justice protects the vulnerable from being sentimentalized and then abandoned.
- Mercy protects the vulnerable from being crushed by the coldness of rules.

Justice without mercy becomes cruelty with paperwork. Mercy without justice becomes indulgence that leaves the weak unprotected. *Rahamim* is not "being nice." It is the refusal to let suffering be treated as deserved, invisible, or irrelevant.

The modern world is increasingly good at administration and increasingly bad at compassion. Systems process cases; they do not "see" persons. Artificial intelligence can optimize outcomes, but it cannot feel the ache that compassion names. It can calculate tradeoffs, but it cannot grieve. Judaism insists that a society that loses *rahamim* does not become more rational—it becomes less human.

---

22   Babylonian Talmud, *Shabbat* 151b,

Chapter Twelve

Gratitude

Judaism begins the day not with ambition but with thanks.

Before any commandment is fulfilled, before any task is undertaken, the Jew is taught to say: *Modeh Ani*—I thank You[23]. The first act of consciousness is not control, but acknowledgment of having been entrusted—again—with life.

Gratitude in Judaism is not polite etiquette. It is moral orientation.

To give thanks is to recognize that one's life is not self-generated. Breath, time, strength, relationships, opportunity—all arrive before they are earned. Gratitude names this asymmetry. It teaches the human being to stand in the world not as owner, but as beneficiary; not as sovereign, but as steward.

Modern culture trains us to experience life as entitlement. Judaism trains us to experience life as gift.

This difference is decisive. A person who experiences the world primarily as entitlement tends toward resentment: whatever is missing

---

23 The brief prayer *Modeh Ani* has its origin in the Talmud *Berakhot* 60b: "*My God, the soul You placed within me is pure… Blessed are You, who restores souls to lifeless bodies.*" The rabbinic understanding is that sleep is a partial death and awakening a kind of resurrection (*Berakhot* 57b). Each morning is therefore experienced as a miniature act of re-creation. God entrusts the soul again, despite yesterday's failures. Awakening becomes a renewed moral endowment.
In other words: existence itself is framed as a responsibility loaned daily.

feels like injustice. A person trained in gratitude experiences the world as provision: whatever is present becomes a reason for responsibility.

Gratitude does not deny suffering. It does something subtler and more powerful—it refuses to let suffering erase blessing. Jewish prayer holds both simultaneously: lament and thanksgiving are not opposites. They are parallel forms of truth.

Judaism does not leave gratitude to spontaneous feeling. It structures it.

Blessings are attached to ordinary acts: eating bread, seeing the ocean, waking from sleep, encountering beauty, surviving danger. This is not ritual excess. It is ethical training. The repetition of blessing creates attentiveness. It interrupts the automatic. It restores wonder to what familiarity has dulled.

To bless is to resist the anesthetizing effect of routine.

The rabbis taught that one should recite a hundred blessings a day[24]— not to multiply words, but to multiply awareness. Gratitude becomes a practiced skill.

Gratitude dismantles the illusion of self-sufficiency.

A grateful person knows that talent alone is not enough; circumstances matter. Effort matters; so does timing. Intelligence matters; so do teachers. Health matters; so does care received from others. Gratitude therefore generates humility—not humiliation, but realism about interdependence.

This is why ingratitude is treated so severely in Jewish thought. Ingratitude is not a minor flaw; it is a form of moral blindness.

Gratitude in Judaism never ends with the self. To receive is to become obligated. The logic is simple: what is given to me is not given for me alone. Gratitude ripens into responsibility when it asks: what am I now required to pass on?

---

24   Talmud, Berakhot 43b

This is why Jewish gratitude always bends outward. We thank God not only with words but with deeds—feeding the hungry, welcoming the stranger, protecting the vulnerable, educating the next generation. Blessing becomes mission. A grateful society is not one that feels good. It is one that gives forward.

Judaism binds gratitude to remembrance. The Exodus is recalled daily. Liberation is retold annually. Historical suffering is not erased; it is integrated into consciousness. Gratitude does not mean forgetting pain. It means refusing to let pain be the final word.

The Jew gives thanks not because history was easy, but because survival itself is astonishing.

To be grateful is to remain human in a world increasingly designed to make us forget that we are receivers before we are producers.

PART IV:
SOCIAL RESPONSIBILITY
AND HISTORICAL HORIZON

Chapter Thirteen

Tzedek

Justice, Justice Shall You Pursue

Judaism does not treat injustice as an inconvenience. It treats it as a catastrophe.

Not only because injustice harms people—though it does—but because it threatens the moral intelligibility of the world. If cruelty prevails with impunity; if the innocent suffers without meaning; if power replaces right—then existence becomes arbitrary. Biblical faith refuses that conclusion. It insists that the world is answerable.

That is why the Torah does not say: *Be just when you can.* It says: *"Justice, justice shall you pursue.*[25]*"* Justice is not an ornament of social life. It is the condition of a livable world.

The Hebrew tradition uses two terms that overlap yet are not identical.

Mishpat most often refers to *judgment, law, the court's decision, the lawful order*—justice as *structure* and *adjudication*.

Tzedek / tzedakah refers to *rightness, righteousness, fairness*—justice as *moral substance*, the demand that human life be safeguarded in dignity.

In practice they intertwine. But the difference matters: a society may

---

25 Deuteronomy 16:20

have *mishpat* (courts, statutes, procedures) while lacking *tzedek* (fairness, protection of the vulnerable, truthful moral discernment). The Torah refuses to let legality exhaust justice.

The biblical dream of justice is never merely mechanical.

Solomon prays not for power, and not even for strict knowledge of law, but for *"an understanding heart... to discern between good and evil.*[26]*"* Justice demands a human subject capable of judgment. One must see more than categories—more than "right/wrong," "guilty/innocent." One must perceive the human reality at stake.

This is why Jewish justice is not only *procedural* (how to decide), but *substantive* (what life must look like if it is to be worthy of God's world). It asks: Are people fed? Are workers paid? Are widows protected? Are strangers safe? Do the poor have access to "food and clothing"—the Torah's blunt material language for dignity?

When God draws Abraham into the decision about Sodom, Scripture gives a reason: Abraham is commanded to teach his descendants *to do tzedakah and mishpat*[27]. In other words: he is being trained—and training the future people—to participate in moral evaluation, not merely to obey.

This is the revolutionary claim: justice is not only something God performs *on* the world. It is something God calls human beings to enact *with* Him. Not because God lacks power, but because a moral world requires moral agents.

The prophets do something even stronger: they link justice to sanctity.

God is *"sanctified through righteousness"* and *"exalted through justice.*[28]*"* Holiness, in this view, is not escape from the social world. It is the moral quality of the social world when it reflects God's will.

---

26 First Book of Kings 3: 9

27 *Genesis* 18: 19

28 *Isaiah* 5:16

That is why "*Be holy*" is surrounded by laws about wages, property, speech, the vulnerable, and the stranger. Holiness is not only what happens in the sanctuary. It is what happens at the gate, the field, the marketplace, and the employer's desk.

Paganism (and modern secular cynicism) can shrug: the world is conflict; the strong win; the weak suffer. Biblical faith cannot shrug. If there is One God—if reality is not morally indifferent—then injustice is a scandal that provokes protest, argument, and prayer. That is why Jeremiah, the Psalmists, Job, and Jonah all force the question. The Jewish people do not "make peace" with injustice—even while believing in providence.

This is not naïveté. It is the refusal to normalize moral chaos.

The prophets confront a painful truth: injustice can become legal.

As land shifts from small holders to elites; as courts become purchasable; as debt becomes slavery; as "legal" mechanisms are used to dispossess—justice is commercialized. The rich can afford more "justice" than the poor.

The prophetic protest is not anti-law. It is anti-corruption, anti-capture, anti-idolatry of legality. A society may follow procedure while crushing persons. The Torah and prophets call that a betrayal.

Love can supplement justice but cannot replace it. Mercy without justice becomes indulgence toward the cruel—"kindness to the cruel is cruelty to the kind."

Judaism insists on both: law and compassion, justice and *hesed, tzedek* and *rahamim*. But the order matters: without justice, compassion becomes sentimental; without compassion, justice becomes cold and destructive.

Technological civilization accelerates decisions, fragments responsibility, and turns moral questions into administrative workflows.

In such a world, justice is threatened in two ways:

1. Reduction to compliance (if the system is "within policy," it is

considered moral).

2. Replacement of judgment by automation (if the model outputs a recommendation, the human abdicates discernment).

Judaism rejects both. Justice requires a human being who can answer—who can be questioned, who can repent, who can change. No system can inherit that burden.

Justice, justice shall you pursue—means: you do not outsource the moral core.[29]

---

29 The Rabbinic tradition notes the doubling "justice, justice" in *Deuteronomy* 16:20 emphasizes both *the goal and the means*: justice must be sought not only in outcomes, but in the way it is pursued.

Chapter Fourteen

Emet

Is this person trustworthy?

Judaism does not begin by asking, "Is this statement accurate?" It begins by asking, "Is this person trustworthy?"

In Hebrew Scripture and rabbinic tradition, truth is not first an epistemological category. It is a relational virtue: fidelity to one's word, reliability over time, speech that matches intention, testimony that bears the weight of consequence.

Emet (Truth) is the bond that allows human beings to live together without fear—and to stand before God without duplicity.

Truth in this tradition is not primarily correspondence between statements and facts. Truth is faithfulness — reliability in relationship. Human truthfulness means honoring one's word, acting with integrity, sustaining trust.

The Western philosophical tradition, by contrast, tends to treat truth as a property of propositions: the *correspondence* between claim and object, or the *coherence* of claims within a system of knowledge. That framework is powerful—and Judaism does not reject it. But it is not the center.

The Hebrew word *emet* (truth) shares its root with *emunah* (faithfulness). Truth is relational before it is theoretical.

Truth, here, is not "what matches an object." There *is* a biblical and halakhic concern for factual truth: investigating, interrogating, establishing a matter. Courts require evidence. Witnesses must be precise. "If it is true, the fact established..."

But the deeper Jewish claim is that truth is speech that keeps faith. Saying with the lips what one says in the heart, quoting correctly, honest commerce, abstaining from deceit and hypocrisy. Truth is character made public.

Truth, however is not the only value. Judaism binds truth to other moral realities:

- truth and peace
- truth and justice
- truth and righteousness
- truth and grace/hesed
- even truth and salvation

Because there are also moments when "the truth" is spoken not to heal but to humiliate, not to clarify but to wound, not to serve reality but to serve the ego of the speaker, Judaism insists that speech must be accountable to what it produces in human life. Not every accurate statement is righteous. Not every disclosure is holy. Truth belongs to the covenantal fabric of trust; when truth is used to tear that fabric, it has lost its purpose.

This is not permission to lie as convenience. It is a demand to treat speech as moral action. Words create worlds. Speech must sometimes be governed by mercy, restraint, and tact—not because truth is worthless, but because life is precious.

This is not relativism. It is moral seriousness. Sometimes, absolute candor can be a form of cruelty. Sometimes, "telling the truth" is a weapon. Judaism therefore insists that truth on earth must be humanly responsible truth—truth that does not destroy the goods it was meant to serve.

This is one of the great Jewish correctives to fanaticism.

> *"When God came to create Adam, the ministering angels formed opposing groups. Love said, "Create him, for he will perform deeds of love." Truth said, "Do not create him, for he is all falsehood." Righteousness said, "Create him, for he will perform righteous deeds." Peace said, "Do not create him, for he will be full of strife."*
>
> *What did God do? He took Truth and cast it to the earth...*"[30]

Meaning: human life cannot be sustained by "heavenly truth"—pure, total, unbroken. That kind of truth, in human hands, becomes tyranny. People kill because they imagine they possess the whole.

So God gives human beings a different task: not to *possess* truth, but to gather its fragments, to repair trust, to test claims against experience, to learn modestly, to correct. Truth on earth is therefore partial, fragile, contested, dependent on character Not because truth is unreal—but because human beings are.

Truth is not merely something we know. It is something we are—or fail to be.

---

30   Genesis Rabbah 8: 5

Chapter Fifteen

Tikvah

Not A Mood, A Moral Will

Judaism's optimism is not the temperament of someone who expects life to be easy. It is the discipline of someone who refuses to let evil have the last word.

That is why one can call Judaism "the religion of ethical optimism"—but only if we immediately clarify what kind of optimism this is: not the naïve belief that "things will work out, not a secular utopianism that imagines progress is automatic, but a a confidence shaped by Jewish responsibility and the knowledge of where one comes from that the good is *real*, that human choice matters, and that history is accountable to a moral demand beyond power.

The Bible begins with a metaphysical wager: existence is not a mistake.

Creation is declared good—not because the world is painless, but because reality is not governed by nihilism. That starting point generates a moral consequence: if the world is God's work, then withdrawal is not holiness and resignation is not wisdom.

That is why Judaism consistently resists the idea that the root of life is evil, or that humanity is incurably corrupt by "original sin." It expects sin, it names it, it punishes it, but it does not worship it as destiny.

Jewish hope is not primarily a feeling. It is an action-structure.

"You shall..." is the hidden grammar of Jewish optimism. The mitzvah assumes that a future exists that can be shaped; that human beings can choose; and that God demands the dignity of agency.

Even when the tradition is brutally honest about human evil, it keeps returning to the same refusal: you are not excused. That refusal is optimism—because it treats human action as meaningful.

Judaism does something more difficult than cheerfulness: it builds a way to live without lying about the darkness.

The classic tension becomes:

> Creation's goodness vs. history's cruelty; moral liberty vs. the apparent success of evil

The tradition's answer is not a single formula. It is an ensemble of protest and prayer, law and repair (*tkikun*), discipline and mercy, and—always—messianic horizon (not as prediction, but as moral insistence that justice is not a fantasy).

"For two and a half years the School of Shammai and the School of Hillel disagreed.

These said: *It would have been better for man not to have been created than to have been created.*

And those said: *It would have been better for man to have been created than not to have been created.*

They finally took a vote and concluded:

It would have been better for man not to have been created than to have been created.

abstractly, it might have been better not to have been created; but now that we exist, we must examine our deeds."[31]

This is Jewish realism at full strength: life is not romanticized, suffering

---

31   Talmud, Eruvin 13b

is not denied, and yet responsibility is reaffirmed.

That "*and yet*" is precisely Jewish optimism: we do not sanctify despair as depth.

The tradition's iconic motto—associated with Nahum of Gimzo[32] (*Gam zu l'tovah*, "This too is for the good")—is often misunderstood as a claim that everything is obviously good.

It is stronger and more ethical than that: It does not say: "Everything is fine." It says: "Even when this is not fine, the story is not finished—and I will not give evil the authority to define reality."

Likewise Rabbi Akiva: "*Whatever the Merciful One does is for the good.*[33]" That is not a sentimental slogan. It is a covenantal stance against meaninglessness.

Judaism is optimistic because it is not escapist. It looks at evil straight on—and still insists on covenant, law, repair, and future.

That is why one of the sharpest Jewish critiques of modernity is that it confuses hope with inevitability. Jewish hope gives no blank check to history.

Judaism "invents" the future as a moral category. The future is not

---

32 Ta'anit 21a. It's illuminating to read Nahum of Gimzo alongside the famous dispute between the schools of Hillel and Shammai. Hillel–Shammai articulate the *burden of existence*: human life is morally dangerous. Creation itself imposes accountability. Once here, the human being must engage in constant self-examination. Nahum of Gimzo embodies the *stance within that burden*: even when events appear catastrophic or absurd, one does not relinquish agency or trust. *Gam zu l'tovah* is not naïve optimism; it is disciplined refusal to interpret suffering as moral meaninglessness. Judgment must not collapse into despair. Even under radical uncertainty, one remains obligated to respond with faithfulness and moral steadiness.

Togther, Hille-Sahhai and Nahum of Gimzo , they express a core Jewish intuition that human life is not justified by comfort or success, but by responsibility — and responsibility must be sustained even when circumstances seem to contradict it.

33 Talmud, Berakhot 60b

merely what will happen; it is what should happen.

That yields two distinctive features: no fetish of the present-today is not ultimate; no worship of progress. Betterment is possible, but never automatic; it requires moral will, institutions, learning, restraint, and justice.

So, Jewish optimism is not "everything will be okay." It is: *it is forbidden to stop trying.*

Jewish optimism is not the smile of someone who expects a smooth road. It is the walking. It is the belief that creation is worth saving, that human beings are answerable, and that justice is not a decorative idea but a promise woven into the structure of covenant and time. Or, in the most Jewish form of the thought:

> *We do not know what will happen.*
> *We know what we are commanded to do.*

Chapter Sixteen

Israel's Mission to Humanity

Judaism lives inside a creative tension.

On one side stands *particularism*: the thick bonds of peoplehood—language, memory, covenant, obligations to "our own," and the hard-earned instinct of continuity.

On the other stands *universalism*: the insistence that God is not a tribal deity, that every human being bears divine image, and that Jewish faith must speak to the moral condition of humanity.

Both elements are native to the tradition. The crisis begins when we turn the tension into a choice.

A great internal crisis in Jewish life today is precisely a loss of balance between these two commitments. One response—often intensified by historical trauma—tightens Jewish identity into defensiveness: a barricaded Judaism, suspicious of the world and tempted toward religious tribalism. The other response dissolves Jewish identity into vague humanitarianism: so open to the world that it risks fading out of the Jewish story altogether.

Particularism is a Jew's primary attachment to and concern for other Jews—continuity, mutual responsibility, shared fate. Universalism is a parallel attachment to the causes of humanity in general—dignity, justice, compassion, and the moral repair of the world. There need be no conflict—unless the two are severed.

If there is no link between the universal and the particular, Judaism breaks asunder: pure particularism becomes spiritual narcissism, pure universalism becomes a lifeless abstraction.

The tradition can speak of Israel as chosen without concluding that only Jews stand in relation to God. Israel is tasked to become "*a priestly kingdom and a holy nation,*[34]" not as a badge of superiority, but as a vocation of service—"*a light unto the nations,*" and a conduit of blessing to "all the families of the earth."

That is the key: *Jews are withdrawn from mankind in order to serve it.* Not to escape the human condition, but to accept responsibility inside it. We become universal by being faithful to our particularity.

Only if we preserve the sanctity of the family can we speak authoritatively about family.

Only if we keep Shabbat can we say something original about work, rest, limits, and the dignity of human non-productivity.

Only if we live a covenantal moral discipline can we offer the world more than opinions.

It is only by being different that we have something different to contribute.

A Judaism that tries to universalize itself by flattening its distinctiveness will have nothing to give but ideas borrowed from contemporary secular liberal culture and then reheated and repackaged as Judaism — without adding anything distinctively Jewish. A Judaism that preserves itself by hardening into exclusion will betray its own God—who is the Creator of all.

The Hebrew Bible itself stages the relationship.

It begins with Adam, not Abraham: the archetype of humanity, shaped from *adamah*—earth. The opening chapters of Genesis are not tribal origin stories; they are claims about the whole human race. Even the

---

34 *Exodus* 19:6

Jewish New Year, in its theological meaning, gestures toward the birth of the world and humanity—not toward a narrowly Jewish event.

Then comes Abraham and covenant: not a retreat from humanity, but a strategy for serving humanity through a particular people living a particular discipline.

Even when the prophets sound universal notes, they often keep them anchored in Zion—universalism with a center. In exile, universal language can become more decentralized—prophecy speaking to and about a world beyond land and temple. After exile, there are renewed attempts to recentralize.

A Jewish hospital differs from a Catholic one in symbols and personal religions, but not in procedures of care. That line matters because it clarifies what universalism is *not*.

Universalism is not erasing distinctiveness. It is acting from it. The world does not need a "universal Judaism" stripped of its practices and obligations. It needs Jews who bring a disciplined moral tradition into public life with humility and competence.

That is why Judaism "belongs to the human conversation"—not as a private ethnic drama, but as a public moral language.

The more Jews are pressed and harried, the more the particularistic element tends to dominate. That is not hard to understand. But it becomes dangerous when fear is enthroned as theology.

We have responsibility to our own people—and responsibility to the world.

The purpose of our commitment to Jewish continuity may be precisely this: to guarantee that the Jewish people who survive can turn to their universal task—effecting God's will for justice and goodness throughout God's world.

Judaism is not tribalism with prayers. And it is not humanitarianism with Hebrew. It is a covenantal people whose particular discipline is meant to generate universal responsibility.

To be a Jew is not to *"dwell alone.*[35]*"* It is to stand in the middle: loyal to a people—and accountable to humanity.

---

35 *Numbers* 23: 9

Chapter Seventeen

Shalom

Peace as Wholeness, Not Weakness

We speak of peace as if it were merely the opposite of war. But Judaism does not treat peace as a pause between conflicts, a diplomatic convenience, or the emotional state of those who have decided not to fight. *Shalom* is a far larger word. It means *wholeness*—a state in which life is not broken into hostile fragments, and in which what is separate can nevertheless belong together.

That is why shalom in Jewish sources can name prosperity and security, harmony and repair, justice and reconciliation, the end of enmity and the beginning of blessing. Peace is not simply an "absence." It is a presence: the positive condition in which a human being, a household, a community, and even the world can hold together without tearing itself apart.

Judaism's passion for peace is therefore not sentimental. It is structural. Shalom is what makes a life livable.

The Hebrew root behind shalom carries the sense of *completion*: to make whole, to restore, to bring to integrity what is cracked or missing. Shalom is not only what you have when you stop fighting; it is what you have when what was damaged is mended, when relationships regain stability, when a society becomes again a place where trust can grow.

That is why shalom is used in Scripture in ways that do not sound "political" at all. It can describe wellbeing, order, prosperity, or security—circumstances unblemished by defect.

In Hebrew, *shalom* does not mean merely peace. It derives from *shalem*—wholeness, completeness, integrity. To greet someone with *shalom* is to ask after the condition of their life as a whole: *Are you holding together? Is your world intact?* It assumes that human beings are not fragments, but moral unities whose bodily, social, and spiritual dimensions belong together. To ask after someone's peace is to ask: *Is your life intact? Are you holding together? Are things well with you?*

In this sense, shalom is not weak. It is the condition for strength. The person who is whole can act. The community that is whole can endure. The world that is whole can bear meaning.

One of the most revealing uses of shalom in the Bible is covenantal. The "peace" secured by covenant is not a mood; it is the integrity of a relationship—an equilibrium, a balancing of claims and needs between two parties. It is legal and moral structure, not vague harmony.

A covenant establishes a foundation on which shared life becomes possible. Shalom is the name of that foundation: intactness, orderliness, rightness between parties. The covenant does not erase difference; it holds difference without allowing it to become chaos.

This is why peace in Judaism is never merely private. Shalom is relational by nature. It belongs to the spaces between persons: husband and wife, neighbor and neighbor, tribe and tribe, nation and nation. It is the moral architecture of coexistence.

Jewish literature contains exalted hymns to peace. It also contains war laws, battle narratives, and fierce moral realism. The tradition does not pretend that Israel floated above the violence of history.

Ancient Israel was born amid violence—as were most peoples. Even the biblical authors, when they imagine "peace," sometimes imagine it from the standpoint of victory: an enemy subdued, threats removed, order restored. That fact should not surprise us. People who have been endangered often dream first of safety.

But Judaism does not stop there. It refuses to glorify war as a norm. It disciplines power and presses toward a different horizon: a world in which peace is not simply dominance, but reconciliation; not merely quiet, but justice; not simply survival, but blessing.

The point is not to sanitize the tradition. The point is to name its moral project honestly: shalom is the aspiration that refuses to become naïve.

In rabbinic sources, shalom becomes explicitly an ethical category: overcoming strife, preventing enmity, repairing social fracture. The sages praise peace relentlessly. Some even declare that the Torah itself was written "for the sake of peace."

But the same tradition also teaches a hard truth: values collide. There are moments when peace clashes with strict justice, and even with strict truth. Judaism does not solve these collisions by declaring one principle absolute. It solves them by insisting on judgment, responsibility, and context.

A famous rabbinic claim crystallizes the tension:

> *Where there is strict justice, there is no peace;*
> *where there is peace, there is no strict justice.*[36]

This is not cynicism. It is realism. Strict justice can become socially explosive—especially when it refuses to consider human limits, communal survival, and the slow labor of repair. For that reason, the tradition develops the practice of compromise in legal settings: justice tempered so that society does not shatter.

And yet Judaism does not allow peace to become a disguise for cowardice or corruption. Alongside its devotion to reconciliation, it preserves another uncompromising voice: *"Let justice pierce the moun-*

---

36 *Midrash Tanhuma*, Parashat Shoftim, §8 and Jerusalem Talmud, Sanhedrin 1:1

tain.[37]" There are moments when compromise becomes a betrayal of the innocent, a protection of the cruel, a quiet surrender of moral responsibility.

Jewish tradition refuses a single formula. It demands a conscience capable of discernment—able to recognize when peace represents genuine repair, and when "peace" is merely the silence of injustice. It even acknowledges that one may, at times, bend strict truth for the sake of peace. But it never permits peace to replace responsibility.

For this reason, Judaism offers two archetypal models of moral response, and it preserves them precisely because their tension is uncomfortable.

Aaron[38] represents peace-making through repair. He enters conflict personally. He pursues reconciliation, lowers shame, restores dignity, and opens paths back to relationship. His approach assumes that many human quarrels are not destined to harden into permanent division. They can be softened by humility and healed by bringing people back into their better selves.

Phinehas embodies a darker truth[39]. There are crises in which peace

---

37 Talmud, Sanhedrin 6b

38 This portrait of Aaron (Moses' brother and High Priest) draws on *Pirkei Avot* 1:12 and *Avot deRabbi Natan* (ch. 12), describe Aaron as a moral archetype, one who actively pursued peace by mediating conflicts, restoring relationships, and reducing shame between estranged individuals.

39 Phinehas appears in the Book of Number, chapter 25. The episode unfolds during Israel's desert journey. A public breakdown of moral order erupts when an Israelite leader openly brings a Midianite woman into his tent, in full view of the community, at a moment when the people are already reeling from idolatry and sexual misconduct. The act is not private transgression but symbolic defiance—an unraveling of communal boundaries at the center of the camp.
    While Moses and the elders stand paralyzed, Phinehas, grandson of Aaron the High Priest, acts. He takes a spear, enters the tent, and kills both individuals. The biblical text then states that his action halts a plague that had already begun spreading through the people, and God grants Phinehas a *"covenant of peace"* (*brit shalom*) in response.

cannot be achieved through persuasion alone, because the source of strife is not misunderstanding but moral corrosion. When wrongdoing becomes public, contagious, and destructive of communal integrity, delay itself becomes complicity. In such moments, the tradition suggests, love may require decisive action to halt a collective unraveling.

Judaism does not collapse these two models into one. It does not pretend they are equally gentle. It does not romanticize severity. But it preserves both because life contains both kinds of situations. Some conflicts are healed by restoring relationship. Others require confronting and removing a force that is actively tearing the community apart.

The ethical point is not to excuse harshness. It is to insist that peace is not always achieved by the same means.

Shalom is the goal. The path depends on what threatens wholeness in the first place.

Everyone knows Isaiah's dream: *swords beaten into plowshares*[40]. Fewer people remember Joel's bitter inversion: plowshares beaten into

---

The tradition does not present Phinehas as a general model for behavior. His act is treated as exceptional, even dangerous—later rabbinic sources emphasize that such zealotry cannot be legislated and must never become routine. But the episode introduces a hard moral category alongside Aaron's peace-making: there are moments when reconciliation is no longer possible because corruption has become public and structural. In such moments, the text suggests, responsibility may require decisive intervention to prevent collective collapse.

Placed next to Aaron's pursuit of peace and Moses' insistence on justice, Phinehas represents a third register in Jewish moral thought: the tragic necessity of action when persuasion fails and delay would permit further unraveling.

40 *Isaiah* 2:4 This verse is engraved on the Isaiah Wall at the headquarters of the United Nations (on the grounds of the UN Secretariat in New York, near the visitors' entrance). It stands beside the well-known bronze sculpture *Let Us Beat Swords into Plowshares*, making Isaiah's prophetic vision of peace a permanent physical presence at the center of modern international diplomacy.

This is more than symbolic decoration: it is Judaism's ancient moral imagination placed at the heart of global political life — a reminder that peace is not merely the absence of conflict, but the transformation of instruments of destruction into tools of cultivation.

swords[41].

Judaism refuses to become a slogan because Scripture itself refuses it. There are times when peace is the calling of the hour; there are times when defense is. The same tradition that longs for universal peace also warns against moral luxury in the face of slaughter.

That is why Judaism rejects total pacifism as a universal doctrine. It insists that universal peace is the ultimate horizon—but it also insists that protecting the innocent is a duty, and that refusing to defend the threatened can become complicity.

Jewish ethics does not canonize violence; it canonizes responsibility. It seeks a "muscular morality": power restrained by conscience, strength disciplined by the demand to preserve life.

Shalom is not passivity. It is the labor of restoring the conditions under which life can be whole.

And the tradition dares to speak even more boldly: peace is not only a human goal. It is a principle that sustains existence—the reconciliation of opposites without annihilation. In that sense, shalom is not merely what we want; it is what the world *needs* in order to be.

This is Jewish peace: not weakness, but *the courage to hold the world together.*

---

41   *Joel* 4:10 (in the Hebrew numbering of chapters) 3: 10 (in the English numbering. Where Isaiah (2:4) imagines a redeemed future in which weapons are transformed into tools of cultivation, Joel speaks to a moment of judgment and confrontation: a time when moral reckoning requires readiness rather than disarmament.

Conclusion

Responsibility in a Technological Age

This book began with a simple claim: moral life does not start with choice. It starts with being addressed—by the force that rules the universe, by another human being, by a command, by a wound, by history—and realizing that human beings are answerable.

Judaism is the civilization that built itself around that understanding. Not as a theory. As a discipline. Across millennia it trained a people to live without surrendering the idea that human beings are obligated, judged, and summoned to decency.

The modern world has introduced a new kind of pressure against that understanding. It is not only the old enemy—persecution, exile, and poverty. It is something more subtle, a transformation in how agency is experienced. Actions are increasingly mediated by systems. Consequences are increasingly dispersed. Decisions are increasingly automated. Authority is increasingly fragmented. Time accelerates. Responsibility thins.

Artificial intelligence is not the cause of this transformation, but it is its sharpest instrument. It intensifies what modern institutions already began: the relocation of judgment away from persons and into procedures; the replacement of moral language with technical language; the substitution of accountability with compliance.

The danger is not that machines will "become human." The danger is that human beings will agree to become machine-like: efficient, optimized, unanswerable.

Judaism does not offer a new technology, a new policy, or a new utopia. It offers something more basic:

A moral grammar that makes responsibility thinkable again.

A human subject who can say *Hineni*. Not as emotion or identity performance, but as a structure of answerability: I am here; I can be called to account; I cannot hide behind my role, my tribe, my system, or my tools.

A refusal to reduce ethics to a compartment of life. Judaism insists that the ethical is the measure of life itself. It demands that action remain tethered to speech, promise, testimony, and repair.

A civilization of transmission. This millenarian tradition does not trust memory to chance. It builds institutions—the home, the school, the community—to ensure that a people can continue to speak meaningfully, truthfully, and responsibly across generations.

A safeguard against moral monopolies. By distributing learning as an obligation, Judaism prevents the rise of an untouchable caste of the "anointed." It knows that religious elites and technical elites alike become corrupt when they are unaccountable.

The modern world speaks as if ethics were a layer we can add later—after we build the system, after we deploy the tool, after we "see what happens." Judaism reverses that order. It insists that the moral question is primary:

Who will answer for what is done? That question cannot be delegated to a model, a committee, a market, or an algorithmic audit. These instruments may assist human judgment, but they cannot replace the human burden of responsibility, because they cannot suffer, repent, forgive, or repair. Only persons can do that. And where persons refuse to do that, no system will do it for them.

A society that transfers judgment to mechanisms will eventually lose the ability to recognize guilt, name cruelty, or perform repair. It will not become immoral by declaring evil good. It will become immoral by declaring responsibility irrelevant.

This book has also insisted that Jewish modernity contains a paradox. Zionism modernized Hebrew and rebuilt Jewish political power—an extraordinary achievement. But it also carries a danger the attempt to use religious language as merely political language, as if the sacred were neutral, as if words formed in prayer could be safely repurposed as slogans.

The point is not to condemn politics, sovereignty, or the secular. It is to recognize that Judaism is not "religion" in the modern reduced sense. Judaism is a civilization whose language and symbols are charged. They do not become empty on command. A people who treats its deepest words as mere instruments will eventually discover that those words do not obey them.

This is not mysticism. It is moral realism. Sacred language, sacred memory, sacred trauma—these shape a people's conscience. They cannot be replaced by technique without cost.

If the home is the fortress of Jewish continuity, and education is the engine of Jewish judgment, then the future of Judaism depends on whether these institutions continue to form responsible persons rather than insulated identities.

The central challenge for Jewish education is not to "produce Jews" as an outcome. It is to form human beings capable of Jewish responsibility: capable of learning, judgment, solidarity, restraint, repair, and truthfulness.

A Judaism that becomes only ritual without understanding becomes escapism.

A Judaism that becomes only identity without obligation becomes tribalism.

A Judaism that becomes only politics without humility becomes idolatry of power.

Judaism endures when it remains what it was meant to be: a discipline of responsibility under non-chosen conditions.

Judaism's most enduring contribution is not that it offers comfort. It offers accountability. It tells the human being: you are not sovereign, but you are responsible. You did not choose your time, your place, your inheritance, your limitations. But you can still be summoned. You can still answer. You can still repair.

In an age increasingly tempted to dissolve moral life into systems, that insistence is not antiquarian. It is urgent.

The future will belong to those who can still say, without sentimentality and without evasion:

Hineni.

APPENDIXES

Appendix A

Index of Persons

Isaac Abravanel (1437-1508) — Biblical commentator and Jewish political philosopher

Abraham (c. 2000–1800 BCE) — Biblical patriarch and covenant founder

Adam (primeval era) — Biblical archetype of humanity

Jacob B. Agus (1911-1986) — Conservative rabbi and Jewish theologian

Rabbi Akiva (c. 50-135 CE) — Tanna (early rabbinic sage)

Joseph Albo (c. 1380-1444) — Medieval Jewish philosopher

Alexander Altmann (1906-1987) — Historian of Jewish philosophy

Amos (8th c. BCE) — Biblical prophet

Aaron (13th c. BCE) — Biblical High Priest

Leo Baeck (1873-1956) — German Jewish theologian

Yitzhak Baer (1888-1980) — Jewish historian

Ben Azzai (2nd c. CE) — Tanna (early rabbinic sage)

Tsvi Bisk (b. 1949) — Israeli futurist and strategic thinker

Martin Buber (1878-1965) — Jewish philosopher

Hasdai Crescas (c. 1340-1410) — Medieval Jewish philosopher

Abraham Cronbach (1882–1965) — American rabbi and pacifist thinker

David (c. 1010–970 BCE) — King of Israel

Moshe Dror (20th–21st c.) — Israeli futures strategist

Ezra (5th c. BCE) — Biblical scribe and communal leader

Emil Fackenheim (1916–2003) — Jewish post-Holocaust philosopher

Saadia Gaon (882–942) — Gaon and medieval Jewish theologian

Heinrich Graetz (1817–1891) — Jewish historian

Irving Greenberg (b. 1933) — Orthodox rabbi and theologian

Julius Guttmann (1880–1950) — Historian of Jewish philosophy

Habakkuk (7th c. BCE) — Biblical prophet

Judah Halevi (1075–1141) — Medieval Jewish poet and philosopher

Hillel (c. 110 BCE–10 CE) — Tanna (early rabbinic sage)

Samson Raphael Hirsch (1808–1888) — Orthodox rabbi and communal leader

Isaiah (8th c. BCE) — Biblical prophet

Jeremiah (late 7th–early 6th c. BCE) — Biblical prophet

Joshua ben Korha (2nd c. CE) — Tanna (early rabbinic sage)

Reuven Kimelman (contemporary) — Jewish scholar of rabbinic ethics

Maurice Lamm (1930–2022) — Orthodox rabbi and ethicist

Maimonides (1138–1204) — Medieval Jewish philosopher and legalist

Golda Meir (1898–1978) — Prime Minister of Israel

Menachem Mendel of Kotzk (1787–1859) — Hasidic rebbe (Kotzker Rebbe)

Micah (8th c. BCE) — Biblical prophet

Moses (traditionally 13th c. BCE) — Biblical prophet and lawgiver

Appendix B

Index of Concepts

What Are Concepts?

A concept is not merely a word. It is the mind's way of grasping something—an internal structure that enables us to recognize, interpret, and reason about what we encounter. We move from sensation and perception to understanding by organizing experience into conceptual form. In that sense, to "know" is to advance from the immediacy of what happens to us toward an intelligible account of what is happening in the world.

Because human experience is fragmentary and overwhelming, the mind cannot treat each moment as entirely new. It must simplify without falsifying. It does so by building concepts: mental representations that summarize experience and make inference possible. When we apply a concept, we are not only naming something; we are drawing conclusions about it—what it is likely to be, what it implies, and how we should respond.

Concepts are closely related to categories but they are not identical. A category is a grouping of things treated as similar (for example: "tool," "family," "law," "freedom"). A concept is the mental representation that allows us to recognize such groupings and reason with them. Categories organize the world as we live it; concepts are the cognitive instruments by which we form, maintain, and revise those organizations.

For a long time, philosophers assumed that concepts function like definitions: a set of necessary and sufficient features that determine membership in a category. Modern research has shown that much everyday thinking does not work this way. Many categories have fuzzy boundaries, and their members are not equal—some are more typical than others. We readily agree that a robin is a more typical "bird" than a penguin; that a carrot is a clearer "vegetable" than parsley; that some instances are borderline. This does not mean our concepts are irrational. It means the world is varied and graded, and our cognitive economy depends on concepts that are usable rather than perfect.

Concepts therefore do something essential: they reduce complexity in ways that allow action. Categorization is not an intellectual hobby added after experience; it is part of experience itself. We do not first perceive a neutral world and only later label it. Much of the time, the brain is already sorting, selecting, and interpreting, often automatically and unconsciously. Conscious reasoning frequently comes afterward—as an explanation or refinement of what intuitive, embodied cognition has already delivered.

This matters because concepts are not innocent. They can illuminate reality, but they can also distort it. When concepts become detached from the experiences they are meant to organize, they become ideological: they substitute for reality rather than clarifying it. At that point, people mistake conceptual facts for facts about the world. A concept can be a tool of understanding—or a screen that prevents understanding.

This book argues that core Jewish values function not only as teachings but as conceptual anchors: dignity (*b'tzelem Elohim*), responsibility (*Hineni*), freedom as moral formation (Exodus), and accountability (*adam mu'ad le-olam*) are not decorative religious phrases; they are organizing concepts. They shape perception, judgment, and action. They tell us what kind of beings human beings are, what kind of freedom is worth having, what obligations cannot be outsourced, and what cannot be done to persons—even in the name of progress.

An Index of Concepts is therefore not a technical appendage. It is an intellectual map. It helps the reader track the book's central vocabulary and see how its key ideas recur, connect, and develop. If the goal is to identify enduring Jewish values without reducing Judaism to slogans or dogma, we must also clarify the conceptual instruments through which those values are understood, debated, and applied. This appendix provides that clarity.

Adam mu'ad le-olam — (קָלוֹעֵל דָעוֹם סָדאָ) — The principle that the human being is always accountable; responsibility is permanent, not situational.

Ahavah (הְבֵהאָ) — Love as commanded action; covenantal attachment extending beyond kin to all humanity.

Anthropology of freedom — Exodus as moral formation rather than political emancipation

B'tzelem Elohim — intrinsic human dignity; universal equality

Bet Av / Bet Avot (תוֹבאַ תיַב / בַא תיֵב) — Household lineage structures; foundations of social, moral, and religious continuity.

B'tzelem Elohim (סיְהֹלֱא םֶלֶצְב) — Created in the image of God; source of universal human dignity and equality.

Chesed (דֶסֶח) — Covenantal loving-kindness; faithful action toward others beyond contractual obligation.

Covenant (תיִרְב / Brit) — distributed responsibility; alternative to sovereignty

Creeds / Dogma (הָנוּמֱא יֵרְקִע / Ikkarei Emunah) — medieval emergence; absence in classical Judaism; limits of doctrinal enforcement

Dignity (human) — (דֹובְכ הֶאָדֱכ / Kevod HaAdam) — non-negotiable; independent of productivity or cognition

Emunah (הָנוּמֱא) — Trust, fidelity, steadfastness; relational commitment prior to doctrinal belief.

Essentialism — search for Judaism's "essence"; critiques of reductionism

Ethical trajectory — continuity of Jewish moral architecture across history

Exodus (מִצְרַיִם יְצִיאַת / **Yetziat Mitzrayim**) — liberation as responsibility; wilderness as formation

Freedom (חוּרֵת / **Ḥerut**) — capacity for answerability, not absence of constraint

Ge'ullah / Go'el (גְּאֻלָּה / גּוֹאֵל) — Redemption and the redeemer; familial and communal responsibility for restoration.

Golden Rule (כָּמוֹךָ לְרֵעֲךָ וְאָהַבְתָּ / **Ve'ahavta le-re'akha kamokha**) — Hillel's summary of Torah ethics

Halakhah (הֲלָכָה) — The "walking" of Jewish life; law as lived ethical practice rather than abstract rule.

Hineni (הִנֵּנִי) — "Here I am"; declaration of moral presence and answerability.

Kavod HaBriot (כְּבוֹד הַבְּרִיּוֹת) — Human dignity; respect owed to every person as a moral absolute.

Mitzrayim (מִצְרַיִם) — Egypt; symbol of constriction and externally managed existence.

Mitzvah (מִצְוָה) — Commandment; concrete act through which responsibility becomes embodied.

Normative Judaism — contested category; limits of lowest common denominators

Responsibility (אַחֲרָיוּת / **AḤrayut**) — personal, irreducible, non-transferable

Systems (institutional / technological) — displacement of agency; automation risk

Talmud Torah (תַּלְמוּד תּוֹרָה) — Study of Torah; learning as sacred obligation and primary religious act.

Teshuvah (הֲבוּשָׁת) — Return; moral repair through acknowledgment, responsibility, and change.

Tikkun (וּקֵּת) — Repair; restoration of relationships and moral order.

Torah (הָרוֹת) — narrative, law, and covenant as moral formation

Yada (עָדַי) — To know / to love; knowledge as relational union rather than abstraction.

Zehut (תוּהֶז) — Identity; meaningful only when joined to obligation and responsibility.

Appendix C

Index of Classical Jewish Texts mentioned in this book

Avot (Pirkei Avot)- Ethical tractate of the Mishnah ("Ethics of the Fathers") focused on character, learning, responsibility, justice, and peace; central to rabbinic moral formation.

Avot deRabbi Natan- a rabbinic expansion of *Pirkei Avot*, elaborating its ethical teachings through stories, dialogue, and interpretation. It deepens themes of character, reconciliation, humility, and responsibility—most notably through portraits of figures such as Aaron as a model of peace-making and relational repair.

Bava Metzia- Talmudic tractate on civil law and interpersonal obligations; includes the famous "It is not in heaven" narrative affirming human responsibility in legal and moral judgment.

Berakhot- Opening tractate of the Talmud, devoted to prayer and daily blessings; establishes practices of gratitude upon waking and throughout ordinary life.

Daniel- Biblical book combining narrative and vision; cited in rabbinic literature for the image of Truth cast to the ground, symbolizing human moral struggle.

Deuteronomy (Devarim)- The fifth book of the Torah, presenting Israel's covenantal ethic in Moses' final addresses; emphasizes responsibility, justice, restraint, education, and continuity over power or sovereignty.

Exodus (Shemot)- Narrative of liberation from Egypt and formation in the wilderness; frames freedom not as autonomy but as entry into covenantal responsibility.

Genesis (Bereshit)- Foundational book of creation, human dignity (b'tzelem Elohim), moral calling ("Ayeka?"), family structures, and the beginnings of covenantal history.

Genesis Rabbah- Classical midrash on Genesis; includes the account of the angels debating humanity's creation and God casting Truth to the ground.

Habakkuk- Prophetic book remembered for reducing Torah's moral core to a single principle: "The righteous shall live by faithfulness."

The Hebrew Bible is the foundational scripture of Judaism, comprising Torah (Law), Prophets, and Writings. It presents Israel's formative narratives, laws, prophetic calls to justice, and poetic reflections on human responsibility. More than a historical record, it establishes Judaism's core moral vision: a covenantal life shaped by obligation, memory, and accountability before God and one another.

Hosea- Prophetic text emphasizing divine compassion; source of the declaration that God desires Ḥesed (lovingkindness) more than sacrifice.

Isaiah- Major prophetic book articulating justice, peace, and ethical worship; contributes to the prophetic condensation of Torah into core moral demands.

The Jerusalem Talmud is an early rabbinic compilation produced in the Land of Israel (4th–5th centuries CE). While shorter and less systematized than the Babylonian Talmud, it preserves important legal discussions and ethical reflections, often emphasizing communal life, social responsibility, and the practical challenges of Jewish existence under Roman rule.

Jonah- Narrative prophet sent to Nineveh; dramatizes resistance to moral responsibility and Judaism's universal horizon of compassion.

Leviticus (Vayikra)- Torah book centered on holiness in daily life; source of "Love your neighbor as yourself" and the insistence that dignity and justice structure communal existence.

Micah- Prophetic text distilling religious life to justice, lovingkindness, and humility before God.

Midrash refers to the rabbinic tradition of interpretive teaching on the Hebrew Bible, weaving legal insight, moral reflection, and narrative imagination. Through close reading and creative exposition, Midrash explores the deeper meanings of scripture, drawing ethical and spiritual guidance from biblical texts and extending them into lived human experience.

Mishnah- Foundational compilation of rabbinic law and ethics (c. 200 CE). It is the earliest authoritative collection of Jewish oral law. Organized by subject matter rather than chronology, it codifies legal rulings and ethical teachings across all areas of life. The Mishnah provides the structural foundation for later rabbinic discussion and serves as the primary framework upon which the Talmud is built. It establishes study, practice, and communal responsibility as pillars of Jewish life.

Psalms- Biblical collection of prayers and meditations expressing trust, moral longing, gratitude, and accountability before God.

Ruth- Narrative of loyalty and inclusion; exemplifies covenantal kindness across boundaries and the moral power of family continuity.

Sanhedrin- Talmudic tractate addressing courts, justice, compromise, and the tension between strict law and peace.

The Talmud is the central compendium of rabbinic Judaism, recording centuries of legal debate, ethical reflection, biblical interpretation, and narrative teaching. Compiled between roughly the 3rd and 6th centuries CE, it preserves conversations among generations of sages about how Jewish law (*halakhah*) and moral responsibility are lived in real circumstances. Far from a systematic code, the Talmud is dialogical in form—presenting arguments, counterarguments, stories, and case studies—modeling a tradition that understands truth as something refined through disciplined disagreement and practical judgment.

Yevamot-Talmudic tractate on family law and relational ethics; cited for teachings permitting deviation from strict truth for the sake of peace.

Zechariah-Post-exilic prophetic book linking truth, justice, and peace and envisioning universal acknowledgment of God.